Thinking Economically

THINKING ECONOMICALLY

How Economic Principles

Can Contribute to

Clear Thinking

MAURICE LEVI

Basic Books, Inc., Publishers   New York

Library of Congress Cataloging in Publication Data
Levi, Maurice D.
  Thinking economically.
  Includes index.
  1. Economics.   I. Title.
HB71.L53   1985   330   83–46090
ISBN   0-465-08553-9 (cloth)
ISBN   0-465-08554-7 (paper)

To Adam, my son,

who must do his best with

my Levi genes

"The Theory of Economics does not furnish a body of settled conclusions immediately applicable to policy. It is a method rather than a doctrine, an apparatus of the mind, a technique of thinking which helps its possessor to draw correct conclusions."

LORD JOHN MAYNARD KEYNES

"The economic way of thinking . . . resembles a magician's top hat: It seems to be empty; but in practiced hands it produces a fascinating array of surprises. And once you've seen for yourself how it's done, you can go back home and astonish all your friends."

PAUL HEYNE and THOMAS JOHNSON

CONTENTS

ix

Contents

PART III
THINKING BIG
Macroeconomic Reasoning

PART IV
THINKING ALOUD
The Horizons and Limitations of Economics

PREFACE

THIS BOOK was motivated by a desire to show that economics is useful. In particular, this book sets out to demonstrate that economics provides a clearer way of thinking about personal decisions, as well as a clearer way of thinking about our national economic environment.

It might seem remarkable that for such an important subject as economics we would need a book to show how useful it is. Remarkable it may be, but a glance at most of the standard books on the subject would almost certainly leave you wondering what practical value economics has. Many of these books are filled with a jungle of graphs and equations, richly adorned with "good X" and "good Y," abstract definitions, and even the occasional "lemma" or "corollary." Any conclusions reached with all these abstract concepts are rarely compared to the views held by most non-economists. Furthermore, even when traditional books do provide examples, they are likely to involve guns and butter, or carrots and Brussels sprouts, products that consume very little of most people's budgets, and that few people make careful, calculated decisions about.

Economics has a far more practical application than showing how much butter, or how many guns we can make if we all work flat out, or how many more carrots we will individually or collectively eat if they become a little cheaper. It can provide, for example, a way of thinking about whether to buy a new or used car, whether to buy a house, whether to stay at school, whether to spend time selecting stocks, whether to go out for dinner rather than go out to the movies, and so on. These are typical of the examples we select in order to lead into the conceptual ideas found in the standard texts rather than doing it the other way around and providing examples only after dealing with the concepts. Often economists are themselves so convinced of the importance of the subject that they don't feel the need to explain the many valuable applications to others before delving into the concepts and the theory. We start out by considering useful applications of economics before considering the theory and the concepts.

Perhaps the most direct way of showing that economics is useful is to contrast the conclusions reached by thinking as an economist about important personal and national problems with the conclusions reached if we do *not* think economically. The greater the gain in understanding, and the fewer the economic principles we draw upon, the greater the value of applying economics. Therefore, this book introduces each topic by looking at ideas common among non-economists. It then describes the central principles the economist uses and immediately compares the implications of these principles to those reached by not thinking economically. The principles themselves are discovered by consideration of a variety of day-to-day problems faced by individuals as well as by governments.

The principles that are most important to the economist's thinking include the distinction between actual and "opportunity" cost; the method of "discounting" the future; the incremental or "marginal" method of making personal or corporate decisions; the importance of "real" versus "nominal" magnitudes; supply and demand; and so on. Different problems require different doses of the various rules (or "tools," as the economist terms them), but within the toolbag or rulebag the economist carries are the means to shape a large range of complex problems into very neat structures.

The reader may already be thinking that there must be about as many ways to think as there are economists. Indeed, it is not only practicing economists who joke that if you laid all the economists end-to-end they wouldn't reach a conclusion! Still, despite popular satire to the contrary, there is an extremely high degree of agreement in the way economists think, and even in the conclusions they reach. The problem is that when they think alike it doesn't make news, or else the economic difficulties don't stay around. (We hope it's the latter.) The consensus in thinking among economists is attested to by the basic similarity of material covered in economics books written by economists of just about every shade of political belief.

Preface

As the author of a book on how to think as an economist, far more problematic than the fact that not all economists think exactly alike is showing economics as a (social) science. The problem is that while it is a science, applying economics involves a bit of art. What we would like to do is show how to tackle every economic problem with the same set of tools, even though this could be like providing a cook with the same recipe for every meal. A good cookbook contains certain themes—baking techniques, how to make sauces, and so on—yet each recipe is different. And so, while we can teach the economic tools rather quickly, it can take the reader some practice to acquire the art of applying them.

The beauty of economics, and this is what gives new students their greatest thrill as the subject unfolds, is that the common ingredients of the recipes for solving problems quickly become automatic. When the way of thinking has been learned, vast new areas of discovery open up. Newly trained economists can sit back and examine numerous events they previously had no way of tackling. It is our hope that this book will help people achieve the excitement of discovery without ever having to leave their armchairs.

It is just as important for the educated person to know what economic thinking cannot do as to know what it can do. Therefore, with each application of the economist's logic, we present both the nature of the logic, and the degree of confidence we can have in the conclusions reached by it.

We concentrate on those conclusions that can be reached without the help of mathematics or geometry.

This is because most people think without applying these techniques, and if it requires too much mathematics it cannot help us think about day-to-day matters. All ideas are therefore explained here in ordinary English. This makes the book self-contained, allowing it to be read on its own or as a supplement to a traditional text. As a supplement it can motivate the reader by showing the practical value of economics, preventing boredom from setting in before reaching the examples given in a traditional text.

Lester Thurow, a noted M.I.T. economist, tells a story of stepping into a hotel elevator at a convention of academic economists. The elevator was empty apart from its operator and Thurow, but at the next floor a number of economists and a hotel janitor stepped in, the economists deep in professionally oriented conversation. The economists got off before Thurow, who was left with the elevator operator and the janitor. Not thinking that Thurow was also an economist, the elevator operator turned to the janitor and said, "Must be an awfully boring job!" We hope that by concentrating on the practical side of the subject, and identifying how much is gained from thinking like an economist, this book will prove that economics is anything but boring.

ACKNOWLEDGMENTS

THE IDEA of writing a book which, unlike the usual ware, shows the ordinary person how to *think* like an economist was not mine, but was given to me, along with its clever title, by Martin Kessler of Basic Books. It is he who deserves the credit for the original concept, while I must bear the full responsibility for putting it into effect.

I began learning to think like an economist at the University of Manchester, England, and further developed the economist's way of thinking as a doctoral student at the University of Chicago. If I have learned to think as an economist, it is to the credit of my teachers and the body of fine literature on which they could draw.

Since leaving the University of Chicago I have continued to learn and practice thinking as an economist at a number of institutions including the Hebrew University of Jerusalem; the University of California, Berkeley; the Massachusetts Institute of Technology; the National Bureau of Economic Research, Cambridge, Massachusetts; and, for over a decade, the

Acknowledgments

Faculty of Commerce of the University of British Columbia. I am indebted to all these institutions, especially the Faculty of Commerce of the University of British Columbia, for providing the environment in which I could do my thinking.

Unlike the many authors who comment that they would not have begun to write the book had they known what was ahead of them, I can say that this book has been a pleasure. In no small measure this has been due to the help of Martin Kessler and his professional editorial staff.

I have to admit that I would never have considered the challenge of writing this book were it not for my wonderful wife Kate, who typed every word. The prospect of raising to its maturity a book from its embryo was lightened by the knowledge that she would always, lovingly, be helping me make it grow.

PART I

THINKING
POSITIVELY

*Positive Versus
Normative Reasoning*

CHAPTER 1

Thinking Subjectively

What the Economist Thinks About

Q: What is an economist?
A: An economist is a person who deals with num-
    bers and charts, but who doesn't have the per-
    sonality to become an accountant.
                                            Anonymous

The less we trouble ourselves with scholastic enquiries
as to whether a certain consideration comes within
the scope of economics the better. If the matter is
important, let us take account of it as far as we can.
                                            ALFRED MARSHALL

ECONOMISTS have a jargon and a way of thinking that
is all their own. When people find themselves listening to
an economist's arguments, and when they can follow the
arguments, they can be fascinated by the way the economist
constructs comprehensive order out of what often appears
as a chaotic assortment of events. However, the fascination
can turn to frustration when the non-economist cannot
follow the arguments, or reconstruct them afterward. This
book is designed to help avoid this frustration and to
provide the reader with a comfortable feeling for the way

economists think. It does not take long to discover that the economist's approach is marvelously straightforward, and yields insights and predictions that would not generally be apparent to the untrained mind.

Economists are by no means the only people to have their own way of thinking about ordinary, everyday events around them. Those in other disciplines also think about what they observe within the frameworks of what they practice. A physicist, for example, who sees a foreign sportscar travel by with a roar is likely to think of the motion of the car in terms of the physical principles governing movement. The physicist knows that under the car's hood a carefully timed sequence of controlled explosions is transferring energy held in the form of hydrocarbon chains into the immediate energy of moving pistons. Via the mechanism of gears and drive trains, the motion of the pistons is transmitted to the wheels to overcome gravitational inertia. Aerodynamic principles are applied to minimize drag subject to limits set by ergonomic considerations so that the occupants enjoy a certain degree of space and comfort. Sound waves from the engine reach the physicist with a shift in length and frequency that are responsible for the sense of speed caused by the sound.

A chemist is likely to think of a rather different set of phenomena when viewing the same sportscar. While concerned, like the physicist, with the combustion of chains of hydrocarbons in the presence of oxygen, the chemist is also likely to think of the gases emitted as by-products, and the effects of lead and other additives on the gases produced. The chemist may also show concern for the effect of additives on the power generated, and if he or she can secure a close look, will be interested in synthetic materials used in upholstery, plastic moving parts, acrylic paint, compounds in the tires, and so on.

A sociologist is likely to think of the car and its occupants within the structure of modern society. If the car is expensive, it is likely to signify to the sociologist that the driver is middle- or upper-class, college-educated, upwardly mobile, concerned with social status, and so on.

A psychologist is likely to see the car owner in terms of individual rather than societal characteristics. For example, if the car is flashy and loud it could signify an extroverted individual who may be insecure.

But what is it that economists, who like sociologists and psychologists consider themselves to be social scientists, think when seeing the foreign sportscar? Our answer will reveal the scope of the subject and the topics we tackle in this book.

The economist often starts out by thinking about the factors behind the decision of the car buyer. This is covered by the Theory of Demand. The car buyer is viewed as having maximized his or her satisfaction, or *utility*, per dollar spent. Because the buyer's income is limited, the maximization is viewed as involving the balancing of the satisfaction gained by using scarce dollars to buy this car versus some other car or object. Weighed in the consumer's maximization of satisfaction is the price of gas and the car's fuel efficiency, the price of other models, the impact of an expensive car on the buyer's job status or expected income (why else do real estate agents tend to drive expensive cars?), and so on.

Because the pleasures and conveniences of a car are not all enjoyed immediately but are spread over a number of years, the economist looks at how future benefits can be evaluated in terms of today's values. It is argued that since one dollar invested today might provide, for example, two dollars in ten years at the going interest rate, then two dollars in ten years must be equivalent to about one dollar today. After all, if one dollar can be turned into two dollars in ten years, why not turn two dollars in ten years into one dollar today? In a similar way the cost of running the car, including future gas and maintenance, must all be put in terms of today's equivalent values before the costs are compared to the benefits. By adding the assumption that car buyers are rational, the economist uses the *cost-benefit analysis*—where the decision depends on the costs versus the benefits—to explain how many cars are demanded.

The same principles for computing today's values from future values can be used for making any decision involving future benefits and costs, whether it be the decision to build a new car factory, to invest in auto shares, to buy a house, or to have another child. Even decisions involving education can be made using the principles of cost-benefit analysis because the costs and benefits of education are spread over time.

Those economists in the branch of the subject known as the Theory of the Firm think about how manufacturers determine the quantities to produce and the number of people to employ. Within the constraints set by government regulations of the workplace and costs of production, firms are viewed as rationally selecting the outputs that maximize profits. For example, economists believe that additional cars are manufactured as long as they add more to a company's revenues than they add to their costs because only then does additional production increase profits. As a result of their efforts to maximize profits, firms are thought of as providing what consumers want rather than as telling consumers what to buy. (Economists frequently cite the heavily hyped Ford Edsel, which was a total market failure, to prove this point.)

The economist, excited by the workings of the economic system, marvels at how an overseas car producer would know what a North American consumer wants to buy, and how via shippers, insurers, distributors, and retailers, the car ends up in the buyer's hands. The economist reasons that by observing what car buyers have been seeking, and by employing or developing the required technology, the auto manufacturer took the initiative and risk to convert the buyer's preferences into a tangible object. Similarly, out of an incentive to make a profit, the shipper had space available to move the car to the buyer's country. Insurers, bankers, automobile transporters, and car lot owners were, despite the absence of anyone coordinating the numerous activities, all available for their part. Step by step, the car was produced and delivered without anyone orchestrating the overall operation.

Because no individual or government agency exercised ultimate control over the intricate, involved system of production and delivery, the economist thinks of the outcome as the result of an incredible "invisible hand" that marvelously and quietly guided the operation. This term, which was coined by the eighteenth-century Scottish economist Adam Smith, goes some way toward describing the remarkably deft but totally uncoordinated and unorganized system that is guided by selfish interest, but that delivers to consumers what they demand.

As is well known, when it comes to the price of the car the economist thinks in terms of supply and demand. The economist reasons that only when the price is such that consumers purchase no more or no less than the firm's purposefully chosen output is the price appropriate. If the price is too low consumers will want more cars than are available, and some means of allocating the insufficient supply is required. If the price is too high some cars will go unsold and unwanted inventory will accumulate. Only at the correct price does the automobile market "clear."

Numerous factors could cause the *relative price* of cars to go up or down, that is, for the price of cars to go up or down relative to prices in general. The economist believes that if people earn more they demand more cars, and if more are not produced this will force up prices. In addition, prices of other products, such as the price of gas or diesel fuel, insurance, maintenance, parking, and so on, affect the demand for cars and hence car prices. Relatively fuel-efficient cars may benefit from gas price increases while larger, inefficient models experience declines in demand. Even the value of the buyers' time influences their choice, some economists thinking that when people more highly value their time they will drive faster cars.

Other factors influencing demand and hence car prices include the maintenance record of the vehicle (people with valuable time tend to buy relatively more reliable cars), interest rates, other car prices, and consumers' tastes. Consumers' tastes are thrown in to cover anything that changes demand and hence prices that haven't already been identified.

Prices are also affected by the cost of production. This influences the supply rather than the demand for cars. However, economists do not think of costs being passed on to consumers. Rather, they think of the effect that costs have on the selected output. Changes in costs that vary according to the level of output, like those of raw materials and labor which are called *variable costs,* are argued as having a completely different effect on output and prices to changes in the costs of overheads, like rent and property taxes, which in the short run do not vary with output.

As for inside the factory, economists think about what determines auto workers' wages. They think of wages as the result of the supply and demand for workers, where the supply depends on the workers' alternative employment opportunities, and where the demand depends on employers' evaluations of employees' contributions to company profits.

The relevance of auto workers' alternative opportunities on the supply of auto workers is that each car producer must pay what the other producers would pay or the employees will work elsewhere. The alternative wage is called the worker's *opportunity cost,* a concept met over and over again in economic thinking.

As far as the factors that influence demand for auto workers are concerned, the economist reasons that people are hired if they contribute more to a company's revenues via their productivity than they are paid in wages and other benefits. It is only in this way that they increase profits and are therefore worth hiring.

Like everybody else, economists are concerned with pollution. They know that it is caused both by car producers and car drivers. In the case of car producers they argue that pollution is a cost borne by society that is not generally considered in determining auto output. This, the economist argues, causes overproduction. Similarly, pollution from driving cars is a cost to others that drivers themselves don't pay, causing them to drive more than is socially "optimal."

9

THINKING POSITIVELY

While *microeconomists* think primarily about problems encountered by individual consumers and firms, such as what to buy or produce, whether to buy a stock or bond, and so on, *macroeconomists* think about larger-scale problems. They are concerned with such questions as the rate of inflation and unemployment, the rate of economic growth, the effect of monetary and fiscal policy on inflation and unemployment, the balance of payments, and so on.

Microeconomists tend to share common views and to think alike. However, macroeconomists are divided into schools of thought, with the two primary schools being the Monetarists and the Keynesians.

If we return to our sports car and suppose that its price has increased along with prices of other cars and everything else, Monetarists will think this is because of a growing money supply (consisting of bank accounts and currency held by the public). The Monetarist explains inflation in terms of the supply of money versus the demand to hold it, rather than in terms of the supply and demand for individual products.

The Keynesian, a follower of the ideas originally expounded by the British economist John Maynard Keynes, thinks of inflation in terms of payments between consumers and firms. For example, a Keynesian thinks of funds being paid by consumers to manufacturers as cars are purchased, with consumers, in their capacity as workers or shareholders in the company, receiving these funds as wages or distributed profits. More generally, firms pay workers and the providers of capital who, in their role as consumers, buy the products of firms. The flow of funds between the two sides can continue unchanged as long as consumers spend all they receive from the firms, and the firms pay back to consumers all they receive from them.

A Keynesian thinks that inflation occurs if the flows between consumers and firms and between firms and consumers become unequal. Inflation can happen if consumers spend more than they earn, which they can do by borrowing, or if firms spend more than they receive, perhaps while building a new factory. It can also happen if the government spends more on defense, social welfare, and other such items than it collects in taxes on wages, profits, and so on. When there are insufficient savings to finance all the amounts the public and governments are borrowing and spending, the economy overheats and inflation results. Therefore, the Keynesian is concerned with such matters as the total value of savings and investment, government deficits and surpluses, and so on.

When it comes to unemployment, Monetarists and Keynesians must explain why people and machines are idle while what they could have produced would have been greatly appreciated by consumers. Monetarists think of unemployment in terms of the supply and demand for workers and think that it results because the price of hiring workers, that is, the wage, is too high; at too high wages, more people would like to be employed than firms want to hire, the definition of unemployment. They provide an explanation of why they think inappropriate wages come about, and this involves workers' expectations about rates of inflation that differ from inflation rates anticipated by firms. Keynesians think about unemployment as they think about inflation, namely in terms of the flows between consumers and firms, and believe unemployment results from insufficient demand because people want to save more than firms, governments, and so on, want to borrow. They believe interest rates might not decline sufficiently to keep desired borrowing equal to the savings.

Since the sports car that we began with was assumed to be manufactured abroad, the economist will think about a number of international factors, but rather than list these we should turn to how economists organize their thinking. Is the economist's thinking really economical?

Thinking Logically

The Economic Way of Thinking

> Q: How many economists does it take to screw in a lightbulb?
> A: It depends on your assumptions.
> KATE LEVI

> Against logic there is no armor like ignorance.
> Ancient Saying

ECONOMISTS believe in positive thinking. This isn't to say they are eternal optimists, and indeed they tend to be rather pessimistic folk; it isn't by chance that economics is called the "dismal science." Instead, by positive thinking we mean that economists approach problems with logic rather than merely saying what they think ought to occur. When asked for the effects of a new tax, for example, the economist invariably answers with a series of logical steps based on *assumptions*. This is distinct from *normative thinking*, which occurs when people say they think the tax ought or ought not be increased.

"Ought" statements are based on beliefs, and while these may well be grounded in a vast body of experience, they are not *positive economics*. For this we must formulate questions in a way that allows them to be approached with logic.

It would be wonderful if we could immediately jump into the logic and show how powerful and useful it is. However, we would quickly find ourselves making assumptions and assertions that frequently turn people off economics before they have reached any of its useful conclusions. Therefore, to give the subject a fair chance we should say a couple of words about the way economists use assumptions and test their logic. However, our methodological chit-chat will be kept to an absolute minimum. It's just an unfortunate fact that before we can sample the contents we must read a little about what we are impatient to taste, particularly the economist's use of assumptions.

The fact that economists depend heavily on assumptions bothers a lot of people who feel that if the assumptions sound unreasonable they nullify any conclusions they reach. Criticizing economists for the assumptions they make is, however, inappropriate. Economists should be judged by how well the answers they provide work in practice. The assumptions are only a step in reaching the answers, but if the answers are what we require and they are correct, we should not trouble ourselves too much with the way they were reached. A couple of examples will help substantiate this.

Suppose we are drawing a map of a city or of a small country. For a precise depiction of distances between any two points the curvature of each area on the globe must be taken into account. The shortest distance as the crow flies turns out to be on a great circle of Earth's surface. Well, because it is difficult to build a two-dimensional map that exhibits curvature, many cartographers assume that Earth is flat.

Is the assumption of a flat Earth so ridiculous that we should throw out the map based on this, even before trying to use it for getting from place to place? No, clearly the value of the map for charting short distances is likely to be little affected by what on the surface—sorry, I can't resist—is a ridiculous assumption.

To take another example, suppose that we are asked to develop a computer program that predicts which way a river will flow given the topography of Earth and the source of the river. What we might do is to allow a drop of water, starting from the source, to search in every direction from the point where it is situated, then calculate for each direction the amount of decrease in elevation per millimeter. The drop of water can decide to move in the direction showing the largest drop-off. From each new point the same calculation can be made by the drop of water, and the direction selected. The steps are continued in our computer program until the drop of water has reached the lowest point on the topographic surface.

If we correctly write the program and take account of inertia, we are likely to predict correctly the course of the river. However, in reaching the answer we have attributed a lot of intelligence to what is only a drop of water. We have assumed that in each position it has calculated the largest negative slope and then decided its direction. Indeed, all drops of water have to make the same incredibly complex calculation. But the assumption that the water is capable of making the calculations does not make the computer program of zero predictive value; it should not be discarded without testing.

These examples should make it clear that a strong case can be made for judging assumptions not on the basis of *prima facie* relevance, but by the validity of the explanations they provide. This shows why the selection of assumptions, which must be done ahead of the explanations, is something of an art. Indeed, the role of assumptions can be explained in terms familiar to an artist.

A good artist or cartoonist can often represent a subject with just a few lines. Sometimes these lines cover only a minute fraction of the surface of a canvas or page, yet convey the full feeling the artist wants to reveal. While there could be more information in a full painting or a photograph than in a line drawing, the gain might be minimal compared to the extra effort involved. The assumption is made by the artist that additional detail was unimportant relative to what he or she drew. A good artist has made the correct assumption if we can still appreciate and enjoy what has been created.

An economist, like an artist, uses assumptions to save time and effort while trying to capture the important elements of a subject. Moreover, by avoiding the clutter of the myriad events and individuals that characterize the full picture, and by sticking to only the most important components, the economist can make the sketch of the economy more vivid than a fully detailed picture would be. If the economist is seeking an explanation of the nation's rate of unemployment or inflation, certain factors will be considered as particularly important, such as the value of consumer spending versus saving, government spending versus taxes, the stance of monetary policy, the health of foreign economies, and the confidence of businessmen. These are the dominant lines of the sketch and we are unlikely to describe our subject well without them. However, whether there is a slump in any one industry, in publishing or in the manufacture of slide rules, is itself not too important for the overall rate of unemployment or inflation.

Even when a sketch has been drawn and the decision on irrelevant detail has been made, we may want to examine the importance of this or that line in it. In an economic context we may have assumed that sales of natural gas depend only on the price of gas and of gas appliances, the price of oil, the month of the year, and the level of national economic activity. However, we may want to know how important oil prices are on their own, or how much the level of economic activity affects demand. The economist does this by using the assumption of *ceteris paribus,* which means other things being equal or unchanged. The economist thinks of the effect of gas prices on gas demand while the price of gas appliances, oil, and everything else is assumed to be constant. This doesn't mean they actually are constant. It's just that the economist can think more clearly if each factor is isolated on its own. *Ceteris paribus* assumptions help the economist think about complex, multidimensional problems.

We can think of how economists use the *ceteris paribus* assumption by an analogy with the way police create composite sketches. After deciding that the sketch must include hair, eyes, ears, nose, mouth, and so on, but not the precise position of wrinkles or length of eyelashes, police artists will vary the position of the lines they draw. The lips are made thinner; the ears moved up or down. With each variation, witnesses are asked if the image has been improved. It may be determined that the most important feature is the shape of the chin or the spacing of the eyes.

Along with making assumptions about what factors to consider, and in order to see how they each separately affect the picture, economists assume that people are rational. This allows them to derive a variety of predictions on how individuals respond to particular developments. A rational individual may be assumed, other things being equal, that is, *ceteris paribus*, to select the job offering the highest wage, an amount of rationality that does not trouble many non-economists. However, sometimes the assumption of rationality requires a little more stretching of the imagination. For example, it may be assumed that when the public is holding more government bonds they feel no wealthier because they recognize that in the future they must pay more taxes in order for the government to be able to pay the interest on the bonds.

Perhaps the most common forms of rationality that are met in economics are the assumptions that consumers select from the range of commodities to maximize their satisfaction, and that firms select production levels that maximize their profits. Achieving maximum satisfaction and profits requires a large amount of information that is difficult to obtain. It requires assuming that consumers know the satisfaction they will receive per dollar spent on each commodity or service they can buy, while firms know at what price they can sell extra output, and the production costs of that extra output. Information on these matters is generally unavailable or very costly to obtain, yet economists continue to assume that consumers and firms act as if they had the information. Moreover, it is generally assumed not only that they act as if they had the information, but that all consumers or all corporate managers act in the same way. This is done despite the fact that some consumers might do odd things like make economically bad gambles, and some managers might try to maximize their prestige rather than company profits. But does the fact that people are more heterogeneous than the economist assumes, mean that we cannot proceed with building economic theories? Does the diversity of behavior of individuals and consequent irrationality of some, or all, prevent the convenient grouping of individuals and the building of theories predicated on rationality?

There is no doubt that some people behave differently than those around them, certainly in highly individualist-based Western economies. Therefore, if there is a rational course of action there is a good chance that it is not being taken by everybody or we would not see such diverse behavior. However, economists make the case that the law of averages, also known as the law of large numbers, allows us to legitimately assume that while each person may react differently, a collection of individuals will act in a predictable manner. Indeed, the group may well behave rationally while most individuals constituting the group do crazy things. Let us consider some examples.

It is generally believed by economists that if the price of wheat were to increase relative to the price of other grain crops, farmers would plant more wheat. However, some farmers may do nothing while others may see the wheat price increase as temporary (perhaps due to market manipulation by the Soviet Union) and therefore decide to reduce their planting of wheat. But does this diverse behavior make it incorrect to assume the rational response that links

19

higher relative prices and the planting of wheat? The conventional economist's answer is that the overall response may well still be rational. It is believed that while some farmers may underrespond, or even perversely respond, there are others who may overrespond, and the prediction "errors" are therefore likely to be offsetting.

To show the use of the law of averages with consumers' decisions we can consider the frequently made assumption that consumers spend a predictable fraction of extra income, say sixty cents per dollar of a salary increase. However, the fact is some people may spend the entire extra income while others may put it all into savings. Some people may actually find that the extra income allows them to buy an expensive item they had previously felt unable to afford, and they may add to the extra income from their past savings, resulting in a spending increase that exceeds their increase in income. This may be considered irrational and certainly runs counter to the assumption. However, the economist may argue that provided the average fraction spent by all consumers collectively is not erratic, even if individuals behave differently, the assumption that a predictable and constant fraction will be spent is fine for making predictions about the economy.

As we have stated, the rationality of an aggregate of individuals, despite some irrationality among the individuals themselves, depends on the law of large numbers. Economists also defend the assumption of rationality, especially in the context of the Theory of the Firm, with a principle that is based on survival in a competitive environment.

Efficient firms that make rational decisions vis-à-vis production levels and methods of production are able to cover costs while selling their products at prices lower than those charged by unprofitable and inefficient rivals. Therefore it is argued by many economists that if there is a sufficient number of efficient firms to supply the market's needs there will be no room for the inefficient firms. So when we look at firms that have survived competition they will be efficient firms that make rational decisions; the inefficient firms generally will have fallen by the wayside. While the survivors may not know that they are behaving correctly, they must be acting as if they knew or they would not be survivors.

Rationality, however we explain it, is a *behavioral assumption* the validity of which cannot be tested directly by asking people if they are rational. What the economist must do instead is derive implications of the rationality assumption and then see if they conform with what we observe. An implication of rationality applied to consumers maximizing their satisfaction is reduced consumption of products facing price increases, while rational firms maximizing profits should be observed selecting higher output as prices increase. These implications are obtained via the use of *deductive logic,* involving going from generalities to particulars. (The original rationality assumption itself might have been obtained via *inductive logic.* This involves inducing general rules from observing particulars.) When the implications deduced from the rationality assumption are not contradicted by the evidence, the economist is unable to reject the rationality assumption. "Failure to reject" an assumption is as far as the economist can go since assumptions cannot be proved to be true.

Economists divide factors into those they are trying to explain, which are called *endogenous* or within the sphere of interest, and those they are not trying to explain, which are called *exogenous.* While exogenous factors are outside the sphere of interest they can still affect endogenous factors and indeed, the deductive logic that is central to economic thinking involves seeing how assumed changes in exogenous factors influence endogenous factors. If we are concerned with consumer spending we might ask how a change in sales taxes affects consumption, where the sales tax is determined politically and is therefore exogenous. If we are concerned with unemployment we might ask how a legislated change in minimum wages would affect the unemployment rate.

The implications obtained by applying the deductive logic follow consistent patterns that when learned allow the economist to skip steps. This is what can make the economist's arguments so bewildering to the layperson. By repetition of application, given well-known definitions and commonly made assumptions, certain rules of thumb are clear to the economist and are used without explicitly stating the logic required to reach them. Only by applying the logic in a number of circumstances can the non-economist hope to catch on. However, it is remarkable how quickly the rules of thumb become second nature.

What helps the economist skip steps is practice with the concept of balance or *equilibrium*. An equilibrium is a situation where there is no natural tendency for anything to change unless something explicitly occurs to change it. If farmers are collectively selling all their wheat and no more or less, the price of wheat is said to be in equilibrium; while everything else is unchanged, the price of wheat should remain unchanged. It is only if the output, or supply, gets out of balance with the demand that we are likely to move to a new equilibrium. If the demand exceeds the supply, the equilibrium price is likely to increase. However, when we reach the new equilibrium we should remain there until something disturbs that balance.

There are equilibrium prices, outputs, interest rates, stock prices, and so on. The economic way of thinking means constantly asking, "In what way will the equilibrium be affected by this or by that event, assuming everything else unchanged; that is, assuming *ceteris paribus*?"

The comparison of equilibria is referred to as *comparative statics*. This means the comparison of stable situations, which are, of course, equilibria. For example, the economist might conclude that an increase in the demand for wheat would increase its equilibrium price. This means no more than that the new price after the increase in demand is higher than the old price. The economist is only rarely concerned with the path taken between the old and new price, which is called *economic dynamics*. This disinterest in the dynamics makes economics very different from engineering.

Because the movement between equilibria is relegated to a peripheral part of the economist's mind, the most common approach economists take to solve a problem is to assume we start with an equilibrium. The assumed shock, or exogenous event, is then introduced and the new equilibrium located. The economist might start with supply and demand for wheat being equal, then introduce an increase in demand and find the new equilibrium at a higher price and quantity. Rarely does the economist stop to consider whether the new price and output really are in equilibrium, that is, unlikely to change on their own. The economist is too impatient to jump to the next equilibrium from the next exogenous event.

The economist frequently, and loosely, refers to the behavioral assumptions used in locating the equilibria as the *model.* The model has no physical being and is simply a term used to convey the fact that there is some structure to the way the economist is thinking. Indeed, the models would not warrant space in any magazine other than scholarly economics journals, where they generally appear as rather dowdy mathematical equations or curves in graphical figures. In this form, few people have much interest in the economist's models, however appealing the curves or well-developed the figures. But most of the models do not require mathematics and geometry, these being used only as a short cut when the economist's thinking has many dimensions.

We might point out that avoiding graphical figures and mathematics could result in quite a saving in paper. Economists tend to use an inordinately large amount of paper, especially napkins, diagramming their models for their lunch companions. This habit might have developed as a result of economists' scholarly interest in "free lunches" and indicates they have probably spent little time in more expensive restaurants using cloth napkins. This is supported by the observation that wealthier business and government economists, unlike their academic counterparts, generally do not draw diagrams on napkins, or on anything else.

The implications derived from the economist's models, in other words, the outcomes from comparing equilibria after they have been disturbed by carefully prescribed events, are known as *a priori* implications. This means that they are formed prior to any testing. *A priori* implications are fine if we are interested in making qualitative predictions, and if it does not matter if they are correct. Generally, however, the economist is interested in knowing whether the implications are valid, and therefore whether the original assumptions are valid.

Unfortunately, not only must economists test implications of assumptions rather than the assumptions themselves, but they cannot perform laboratory experiments to generate the evidence to compare with the implications. The economist cannot control the demand for wheat or oil to see if the effect it has on the market price is as the model predicts it will be. Instead, the economist must wait for the demand to change and observe what it does. In that sense, the economist is in a similar position to the astronomer, who must also often wait to test theories—and who may have to wait centuries or millenia. But even when the events needed for testing the economist's theories do occur, they are likely to be entangled within a variety of other events. The demand for wheat might well increase at the same time as numerous other factors occur that affect the wheat demand and wheat supply.

What the economist does to overcome the limitations of not being able to hold laboratory experiments or wait for conveniently uncluttered observations to unfold is to turn to data generated in the past. These data are evaluated to see what happened *on average,* with the hope that the influences of the factors not considered will cancel out over time. When economists do this they are wearing the hat of the econometrician. An econometrician is trained in statistics as well as economics. While every economist learns some econometrics, the subject is sufficiently difficult that certain individuals tend to specialize in testing the theories that other economists have advanced and developed.

Economists' theories that do not stand up to econometric testing are revised or completely rejected. The rebuilt or replacement models are then used until they are in turn rejected or replaced. In this way economics has evolved as a dynamic subject. Sometimes theories survive only a matter of months while others can claim a life as long as modern economics. However, it is the established ways of thinking that we concentrate on here.

PART II

THINKING SMALL

Microeconomic Reasoning

CHAPTER 3

Demanding Thinking

How We Choose What to Buy

> Economists do it on demand.   A T-SHIRT

> Long before Einstein, economists had been aware that Earthly matter has four dimensions: Length, breadth, thickness, and price.
>
> Anonymous

WHEN IT COMES to the decision of what to buy or *demand,* non-economists tend to think of people purchasing what they "need" or "want." A non-economist might say that the number of people seeing—or demanding—a particular movie is determined by the number who think they would enjoy it, perhaps because of its reviews, or the people producing it, or appearing in it.

To the economist, needs and wants have little meaning until they are articulated in a willingness to make a purchase. The economist knows there are thousands and maybe millions of goods and services that we like or want,

29

and for which we may be able to argue that we have a need. However, people with finite incomes and limited time have to give up the opportunity to enjoy other goods or services to enjoy any particular item. Only if a person is willing to buy an item that costs a particular amount and takes up a particular amount of time are wants transferred into what the economist defines as an *effective demand*.

Effective demand refers to the actual quantity consumers would buy or demand at different prices and therefore recognizes that people choose between products competing for their attention. The choice is the result of scarcity of individual incomes and the positive price tags consumers must pay, as well as the limits on their time. The positive prices are themselves the result of the scarcity of products. Indeed, the economist's study of demand is the study of which scarce products people choose given scarce incomes and scarce time.

We can illustrate the way the economist thinks about how we make choices by supposing that you have decided to go out for the evening, either to see a movie or to have dinner. You would like to take your friend. The movie tickets are $5 each; you expect that the dinner will cost about $50 for two.

A non-economist might say that if you have the money, you will do whichever you prefer. The economist would not disagree, but says that how much you want to do each of these activities must be judged relative to their prices. After all, you would probably prefer to eat out for $200, and if you went without something else, and dined this way only rarely, you might even be able to foot the bill. But how much more would you prefer the $200 dinner to the $50 dinner? This is where the evaluation relative to prices comes in.

The economist says that you would choose a $200 dinner over a $50 dinner if you wanted the more expensive dinner at least four times as much as you wanted the cheaper dinner. Similarly, you would eat out for $50 rather than spend $10 for two at the movies if you wanted to eat out at least five times as much as you wanted to see the movie. The economist refers to the amount you want to do one activity versus another as the *relative marginal utilities*. The marginal utility is the satisfaction from an extra movie, dinner, and so on, and the economist thinks we compare relative satisfactions to relative prices. When the marginal utility of the dinner versus the movie exceeds the price of the dinner versus the movie we choose the dinner, and vice versa.

The comparison of relative marginal utilities and prices can be put differently. Instead of thinking of relative marginal utilities and prices we can think of making our choices according to the marginal utilities per dollar from each activity. If the marginal utility per dollar of the dinner exceeds the marginal utility per dollar of the movie, we choose the dinner. But are marginal utilities per dollar things that never change, or do they vary with the amounts that we are consuming?

The economist believes that the satisfaction we receive from seeing a movie or going out to dinner is determined by how frequently we see movies or dine out. For example, if you and/or your partner had been at the movies already that week the marginal utility per dollar of the movie would be reduced and you would be more inclined to go out for dinner.

THINKING SMALL

In case you are a real movie buff or gourmet and feel that you could never become satiated with either activity, let us think of the marginal utility of other products, say for example, cold beer. On a warm day, one glass of beer would likely be far more satisfying than no beers. Two beers per day would be better still, but how much better? If it is twice as good we would say that the extra beer offers *constant marginal utility*. But how about the third, fourth, fifth beers, and so on? Would each extra beer offer as much satisfaction or utility as the beer before?

What the economist assumes is that after a while, increasing the "flow" of beers we drink—the number drunk per day—will lower the satisfaction derived from additional beers. The sixth beer is not likely to be quite as satisfying as the fifth, the fifth not as satisfying as the fourth, and so on. If you don't believe that additional glasses of beer add lower amounts of satisfaction than previous glasses, try rollmop herrings or new shirts. The first herring per day might be considered rather tasty, but how about the fifth? Similarly, one new shirt each month is useful, and so may be the second, but after some level is reached, new shirts won't be of much value. Economists are not saying that they will have negative value (though after twenty herrings a day, or shirts per month, you might develop stomach and/or storage problems). They are merely saying that the extra satisfaction from consuming more will eventually decline. The economist believes that this is true of every product or activity we consume. It is referred to as the *Law of Diminishing Marginal Utility*.

As we have said, the economist's assumption that we select from among various commodities and activities, each with their diminishing marginal utilities so as to maximize total utility, implies that we equate the marginal utilities per dollar spent on each commodity. This is perhaps the most important component of economic thinking about demand, and therefore well worth establishing why it is so.

If we can obtain more marginal utility per dollar from eating out than by going to the movies, we will eat out. However, according to the law of diminishing marginal utility, as we eat out more often we lower the marginal utility per dollar of eating out. At some point, the marginal utility per dollar gained from eating out will fall below that from some other activity, like going to the movies. If we continue choosing between such goods and services, picking those with the highest marginal utility per dollar, we will add to the total satisfaction we receive. We will reach the absolute maximum total satisfaction when all goods and services provide the same marginal utility per dollar because at that point shifting between products cannot result in any gains. Therefore, in order to maximize total utility we should equalize all the marginal utilities per dollar of the different available products.

Economists treat preferences or "tastes" as a given, or in their jargon, as an *exogenous variable*. They believe that people's tastes should not be challenged on ethical or moral grounds, at least not from the perspective of positive economics. Different people have different preferences and therefore different buying patterns, all of which are justifiable to the economist. Some of us will buy lots of record albums before the marginal utility per dollar has been reduced to the marginal utility per dollar for other commodities, while others see a lot of movies before marginal utilities are equalized. There are also likely to be many products each of us does not consume at all because at no level of consumption is the marginal utility per dollar above that of something else.

The economist's way of thinking in terms of equalizing marginal utilities per dollar can be used to explain why most people have only one refrigerator or house. When you have no refrigerator or house the marginal utility is very high. The maximization of total utility therefore involves buying your first refrigerator or first home. However, after the initial purchase has been made the marginal utility drops off rapidly. Other priorities become dominant then and other products are purchased.

Because homes and refrigerators are large and expensive items we cannot vary the number of each in order to make the marginal utilities per dollar equal to those of other products. However, we can vary the size of a home or refrigerator we buy and get very close to equating the marginal utilities per dollar.

We can add another dimension to the economist's way of thinking if we extend the options available in our movie versus dining out example to include earning income. Let us suppose that you have the chance to earn $50 by working at home for the evening if you don't go to see the movie or go out to dinner.

The economist thinks of the cost of what we do in terms of what we are forced to give up. If the choice available were limited to the movie and the dinner out, if we chose to eat out the cost would be the foregone movie. This cost is referred to as the opportunity cost, a concept met over and over again in economics. When we have the option of earning $50, a component of the total cost of both eating out and seeing the movie also includes the foregone income.

This cost must be added to the dollar cost of each activity to come up with the total cost. Consequently, the relevant cost of going out for dinner is $100. This consists of $50 of foregone income and the $50 cost of the meal that represents the foregone opportunity to buy something else costing $50, such as five movies. Similarly, the cost of going to the movies is $60, consisting of $50 of foregone income and $10 of other foregone spending including, for example, one-fifth of an evening out in a restaurant. In general, the opportunity cost is measured as the satisfaction received from the next best alternative available, which involves only working and movies or dining out in our example, but involves a much broader range of alternatives in most situations.

The effect of extending the concept of cost to include foregone income is to change the price ratio or the relative price of movies to dinners out. Before we added the chance to earn $50, the meal was five times more expensive than the movie. The frequency of going out to dinner and to the movies would, therefore, have been adjusted to the point that with diminishing marginal utility of both activities, the marginal utility of dinner was five times that of seeing another movie. However, when we include the foregone income, making the total cost of the dinner $100 and that of the movie $60, the point at which relative marginal utilities equal relative prices involves a completely different frequency of the two activities. Because movies have become relatively more expensive, the frequency of dining out is likely to be increased relative to the frequency of seeing movies. With diminishing marginal utility, this will lower the marginal utility of dining out relative to seeing movies. Only when the adjustment has brought the marginal utility of the dinner down to the fraction 100/60 of the marginal utility of a movie will the choice be correct, that is, provide maximum utility and a new personal equilibrium. This is where the relative marginal utilities equal the relative prices, including the foregone income.

What we have found from adding the extra dimension of economic thinking about costs is that when our time is valuable we are more likely to do expensive things. This is not because having valuable time necessarily makes us richer. Rather it is because it changes the relative costs of activities. It raises the relative cost of what in purely monetary terms may be cheap.

The value of time is an important consideration in many consumer decisions. The inclusion of this cost explains why people generally have searched for faster ways to wash dishes and clothes, for getting from place to place, and so on; time has become more valuable as our wage rates and salaries have increased.

The increased value of our time explains why fast-food outlets and convenience foods have been so successful. As the component of the total cost which consists of the value of time has gone up we have moved away from activities that use a lot of time into activities that economize on time. This explains our interest in air travel instead of ocean or land travel and our preoccupation with being served quickly at the supermarket. It also explains why people in poorer countries, where their opportunity costs are lower, do not appear to mind spending time in line-ups.

You might be tempted to say that the economist goes too far. Maybe it is not the increased value of our time that makes us fly or eat fast food. These products had to be invented before we bought them. While economists recognize that invention is a prerequisite, they will argue that necessity (or demand) is the mother of invention. If we did not value time as highly as we do aircraft would not have been built even if the principles had been known, and we would not have the inclination to eat fast food. Hence these products would not be available if we didn't demand them, and people would not have spent as much effort trying to discover them. The economist believes that everything available is produced only because the consumer is demanding it, whether it saves time or not.

Far more could be said about the value of time in the economist's thinking about the increased use of the telephone versus writing letters and the increased use of urban rapid transit systems versus private cars when city streets become congested. The interest in economizing time has also been behind the growth in popularity of shopping centers, banking machines, self-cleaning ovens, and self-defrosting refrigerators. The value of time can even explain why we spend fewer hours looking for bargains of low-priced items like clothing and food than we do for expensive items like appliances, automobiles, houses, and personal investments. Because the expected savings is smaller on cheaper items, it isn't worth putting in the time to investigate all the prices in town, whereas it is worth the search if it saves $200 on a new car. Indeed, economists will even argue that consumers invest additional time uncovering price information until the expected benefit in savings rewards the time spent.

Because not everyone can earn an income staying at home, let us drop the component of costs that represents foregone earnings and return instead to the purely monetary costs of an evening at the movies or dining out, and ask what happens when these costs change. Let us suppose that movie tickets go up in price to $6 each, or to $12 for two of you.

At the previous frequency of seeing movies and dining out, which was such that the marginal utilities per dollar were equal, you will no longer be maximizing utility—the marginal utility per dollar from movies will be below that of dining out. In order to maximize your total utility you need marginal utility per dollar to be equal. According to the law of diminishing marginal utility this requires a reduction in the frequency of going to movies. This reduction follows because just as increases in frequency lower marginal utilities, reductions increase them. Hence we find that the higher price of movie tickets should cause you to reduce the frequency of seeing movies.

If each of us reduces the frequency of seeing movies when the price of movie tickets goes up then collectively we reduce the quantity of movies demanded. It follows that as prices increase, the quantity demanded in the marketplace declines. This is an essential component of economic thinking on the subject of demand, and should come as no surprise. However, note that it does not come from a direct assumption. We derived the conclusion indirectly via assuming that we individually maximize utility, and that we face diminishing marginal utility for each separate product. These two assumptions produced the implication that we reduce the quantity demanded as prices go up.

You might well be wondering why economists do not just directly assume that people reduce the quantity demanded as prices increase. After all, this is eminently reasonable, so why bother to derive it from other assumptions? Economists answer that they prefer to derive behavior from the most basic assumptions possible. Assuming that we do the best with our limited incomes, that is, that we maximize utility, and that marginal utilities of products decline as we consume more of them, are more basic assumptions than the assumption that people reduce the quantity they demand as prices increase. Moreover, the more basic assumptions provide many other implications.

Let us suppose that the cost of dining out increases to $60. At the old rate of seeing movies versus dining out the marginal utility per dollar of the dinner at its increased price is lower than that of the movie. This lowers the chance of going to dinner and increases the chance you will see the movie. More generally, it reduces the frequency of dining out and increases the frequency of going to the movies. At the lower frequency of dining relative to going to the movies the marginal utility of dining goes up while that of movies goes down, re-equating the marginal utilities per dollar until they are again equal. Therefore we end up satisfied, or in equilibrium, with a lower frequency of going out to dinner and a higher frequency of going to the movies.

We have discovered, not surprisingly, that as the cost of dining out goes up we will see more movies for any given price of going to the movies. We could have assumed this directly, but we obtained it from the same assumptions we used in obtaining the previous conclusion.

In the economist's jargon, the reason why more expensive dining increases the demand for movies is that the choice you are facing between dining out and seeing movies involves *substitutes*. Very loosely, substitutes are alternative ways of achieving satisfaction, such as the satisfaction from spending the evening out. Other examples are butter or margarine for spreads, natural gas or oil for home-heating, cotton or polyester for shirt making, buses or cars for travel, and so forth. In each case, an increase in the price of one of the products will raise the demand for its substitute. This is not the case for all product relationships.

Suppose the price of parking at the movies goes up. The result of an increased cost of parking is, in effect, to increase the cost of going to the movies. For a given marginal utility of the movie, this will lower the marginal utility per dollar of seeing the movie and hence reduce the chance of your going to the movies. Generally, economists argue that an increase in the price of parking lowers the market demand for movies, the opposite to the effect found for the price of dining out on the demand for movies. The reason for the opposite implication is that parking is *complementary* to seeing the movie.

Complements are, defined loosely, items purchased jointly, such as tennis rackets and tennis balls, right and left shoes, cars and gasoline, bread and butter, computer hardware and software, record albums and stereos, video recorders and tapes, and so forth. Complements are the opposite of substitutes in that a price increase lowers the demand for complements but raises the demand for substitutes. Indeed, economists often define what complements versus substitutes are by the direction of these effects. If an increase in the price of a product lowers the demand for another product, these products are often said to be complements. If it raises the demand, they are said to be substitutes.

To distinguish the effects of a product's own price from that of other prices on the demand for the product, the economist uses a different terminology. For example, an increase in the price of a movie is said to "decrease the quantity of movies demanded." However, a decrease in the price of dining out would be said to "decrease the demand for movies." This is a subtle distinction, but it is extremely important to thinking economically. A *decrease in the quantity demanded* occurs as a result of a price increase of the product itself. A *decrease in demand* results from a decrease in the price of a substitute, an increase in the price of a complement, or some other factor.

Changes in quantity demanded result only from changes in a product's price. Anything else that affects demand, whether it be other products' prices, consumers' incomes, advertising programs, tastes, or whatever, will cause changes in demand. One factor that causes changes in demand is consumers' incomes. But how incomes change demands depends on how they affect relative marginal utilities.

Having more income allows people to buy more of everything; therefore, an increase in consumers' incomes generally causes an increase in demand. However, as we buy more the marginal utilities of different products diminish at different rates. The marginal utility of table salt might drop off rather rapidly after you've bought enough to salt your food to taste, whereas the marginal utility from buying more luxurious furniture or a better-equipped car may decline rather slowly. From our previous conclusion, it follows that if utility maximization requires equalization of marginal utilities per dollar from different products, then an increase in income will have different effects on the demand for salt than on the demand for furniture. In particular, after an increase in income the demand for those products for which marginal utilities drop off quickly will increase little, while the demand for products for which the marginal utilities decline very slowly will increase substantially.

Economists refer to goods for which demand increases

minimally from an income increase as *necessities,* and those enjoying large increases in demand as *luxuries.* More precisely, those products for which the spending increases more slowly than income are necessities, and those where spending increases faster than income are luxuries. (In case you are wondering how the amount spent on luxuries can increase faster than income, it is because with the demand for necessities increasing little, income is released for luxuries.)

So far, the conclusions we have reached concerning changes in quantity demanded and changes in demand would not be new to many non-economists. They are intuitively reasonable conclusions, and you might feel that other than the distinction between substitutes and complements and between necessities and luxuries, what we have discovered would have been apparent to any intelligent person. Yet this is not the case for every conclusion reached by thinking economically about demand. Some conclusions would not be reached by many non-economists, even those with considerable intelligence.

For instance, let us consider how an economist would think about the decision of whether to leave a theater after discovering that the movie is terrible, but having been in the theater too long to obtain a refund. Should you stay if you are getting little enjoyment from the show?

The economist reasons that the cost of remaining in the theater is only the opportunity cost of your time. It does not include the ticket price, which is a *fixed* or *sunk* cost; you will pay it whether or not you leave the theater. Therefore, what you must do is evaluate the marginal utility of staying per dollar of your opportunity cost in terms of the value of your time, and compare this to the marginal utility per dollar of leaving the theater and going out to eat or to do something else. It does not matter whether you paid $10 or $100 for the tickets; whatever you have paid becomes irrelevant when you are already in the theater and have sunk the ticket cost.

The somewhat surprising conclusion concerning the irrelevance of sunk or fixed costs can be illustrated by taking another connected example. Suppose that on the way to the theater you discovered that your tickets, which you had previously purchased for $40, were lost. Should this affect your behavior in maximizing total utility? The economist argues that if you had already wanted to see the movie you would buy new tickets, and what happened to the original tickets is immaterial. Let us see how this conclusion is reached by thinking economically.

As we have discovered, the maximization of utility requires the allocation of income between alternatives in order to equalize relative prices with marginal utilities. The loss of tickets does nothing to the relative marginal utilities; it's the same show and same alternatives—eating out or staying home to work. Neither does the losing of the tickets affect relative prices because the price of getting to see the movie after losing the original pair of tickets is the cost of a new set of tickets. As this cost of $40 was originally considered to be worthwhile, it should still be considered worthwhile. There is, therefore, no reason for the utility maximizing individual to decide against seeing the movie simply because the tickets have been lost. The lost tickets represent a sunk cost, and according to economic thinking, this is irrelevant.

We must admit that while losing tickets has not affected the marginal utilities or the prices, it has made you poorer. But you are no poorer than if you had lost $40 in cash in the previous week. The economist therefore says that you are just as likely to buy a new set of tickets if you lost your original tickets as if you had lost $40 in cash. The non-economist may think this violates intuition and indeed, many people, as confirmed by experimental evidence, are more likely to decide against buying new tickets if they lose their original tickets than if they had lost their cash. However, this will happen only if they don't think economically.

As another example of a surprising conclusion from thinking economically about consumers' decisions consider the rationality of going to another gas station to save $10 on a tank of gas, versus going to a different automobile dealership to save $10 when buying a car. The economist reasons that if the value of gas and foregone time to the next gas station or to the other car dealership are the same, consumers are as likely to make both trips to save the $10. All that is relevant is the cost of going to shop elsewhere in terms of time and travel, versus the amount it saves. If the costs are below $10, either journey is just as worthwhile; the benefits exceed the costs. Again, this conclusion may seem surprising to the non-economist who would drive twenty blocks to save $10 on gas, but who wouldn't drive to the next block to save $10 on a $10,000 car.

We have got a lot of mileage from these assumptions, with some intuitive and some unintuitive implications. But how good are the assumptions and hence the implications they generate?

Perhaps the most important assumption we have made is that marginal utility will decline with increased consumption. Because marginal utility is measured for different *flows* of goods—beers per day, dinners out per week, movies per month, or haircuts per year—there is little doubt that marginal utility will eventually decline with increased con-

sumption; we have only so much income and different activities compete for our time. But might we not acquire a
taste for a product? For example, would the assumption of
diminishing marginal utility be violated if by reading this
book you discovered the joys of economics and an increased
utility from additional books on economic subjects? The
economist answers that there is nothing in the assumption
of diminishing marginal utility that prevents people from
changing their preferences over time. Our assumption refers
to a given period of time, and we can be confident that
marginal utility does decline in a given time period as we
consume more and more of a particular product.

A product that comes to mind where an increased flow
could result in extra satisfaction from additional units is
red wine. Many people believe that red wine tastes better
not only after it has breathed, but also after drinking a
couple of glasses. This might explain why some people drink
too much; if marginal utility does not decline consumption
will be large. However, if the disutility of a hangover the
next day is included, people are likely to limit their consumption. Of course, there are those whose utility does not
decline despite hangovers, with many ending up on skid
row or with a serious problem on their hands.

In addition to the assumption of diminishing marginal
utility the economist argues that we maximize total utility.
As we indicated in chapter 2 this assumption, which is based
on rationality, is difficult to check directly. We certainly
will not find out whether utilities are maximized by asking
people if they are doing this. We also won't find out by
asking people if they are equating relative prices with relative
marginal utilities; even professors of economics whose belief
in rationality is paramount do not specifically compute all

the relevant relative marginal utilities. Can you imagine standing in the center of the supermarket surveying all the products to rank the marginal utilities per dollar and then setting off to fill your basket until everything in it provided the same satisfaction per dollar? It is difficult even to know the variety of goods available, let alone the marginal utilities they would provide. But if this is so, how can we be maximizing anything? Economists tend to answer that while people don't calculate the marginal utilities they still allocate their incomes as if they do.

In the case of firms, there are grounds for invoking what is often called the *as if principle*: if firms do not behave as if they are maximizing profits in terms of their output, pricing, and so on they may not survive. The discipline of the marketplace is therefore a reason for the assumed behavior of survivors, even if this reasoning does have numerous limitations. But what is the discipline imposed on consumers? Unlike firms, if consumers do not behave as if they are maximizing their utility there is nothing to put them into bankruptcy or the poorhouse. Therefore, it is difficult to argue for maximization of utility by consumers on the grounds that only the fittest, the maximizers, survive.

Perhaps the most acceptable grounds economists have for their assumptions about maximization of utility and diminishing marginal utility is that the implications of these assumptions generally do conform with what we observe. Recall that with the help of these assumptions we derived the conclusions that a price increase lowers quantity demanded of the product, lowers the demand for complements, and increases the demand for substitutes, and that increases in income have greater effects on some goods than on others. To a limited extent, these implications can be checked against the data and generally fair quite well. Thus, indirect evidence tends to confirm the assumptions we made.

While the economist's thinking on demand does tend to yield useful predictions as far as it goes, there are grounds for arguing that it does not go far enough. This is because of the economist's insistence that tastes are givens.

The economist does not like to deal with people's preferences or tastes. This is motivated by a concern for stepping out of the positive arena and into a moral and ethical quicksand involving judgements about good and bad taste. Does a strong preference for liquor or pornographic magazines constitute poorer taste than a preference for Beethoven and the *New Republic*? Does spending money on stereos and jet-set vacations constitute poorer taste than spending income and time with our children? By taking tastes as given, or in professional jargon, by taking the *utility function* as exogenous, economists rule out the study of these questions.

Unfortunately for the value of thinking economically, tastes do change. Moreover, these changes in tastes represent a part of our economic environment that economics is attempting to explain. We have only to look at the changes in architecture, furnishings, clothing, hair styles, and lifestyles over a twenty-year period to see how quickly tastes change. Moreover, to some extent these changes are brought about intentionally by advertising or may be the result of technological developments, and indeed, the expenditure of billions of dollars on both of these offers evidence that tastes do change. But some changes, whether induced by advertising or not, probably have to do with an innate human desire for change—if you have looked a certain way or furnished a certain way for so long, it's time for a change.

Economists leave the study of the determination of what

is behind changes in taste to others. The study of the effects of advertising is left to professors of psychology and marketing experts, who generally pay about as much attention to economics as economists pay to psychology and marketing. Indeed, it is an unfortunate fact that few economists have shown interest in this purely behavioral side of the subject. Consequently, what many non-economists think economics can help them explain, like why certain products have been successful and others failures, or why the government uses tax deductions to subsidize home ownership and children but not cars and stereos, turn out to have been issues considered too hot to handle by economists.

CHAPTER 4

Thinking Ahead

How to Make Investment Decisions

> We first survey the plot, then draw the model; ...
> Then must we rate the cost of the erection;
> Which if we find outweighs ability,
> What do we then but draw anew the model ...
> WILLIAM SHAKESPEARE
Henry IV, Part 2
Act I, Scene iii

MOVIES or dinners out, the original focus of the choice tackled with economic thinking in the previous chapter, are nondurable. This is not to say that the enjoyment of the movie or satisfaction/indigestion from the dinner will not be with you for some time. Rather, by nondurable we mean that the benefits or costs derived are obtained more or less immediately. This is quite different from the situation with, say, buying an automobile or continuing your education. The "purchase" of these *durable* items provides benefits and costs over many years, which is why the economist calls them durables. The benefits and costs have to be added up and compared; hence the economist has been forced to develop a special way of thinking about the demand for durables.

Non-economists might use the same sort of thinking on whether to buy a new car or whether to get more education, as they would for nondurables. Again, the criterion is likely to be "wants" or "needs," with the need or want for a car being based on the condition of your current car, and the need for further education being based on whether it might provide a better job.

As with all goods or services, the economist recognizes that because income and time are scarce we must choose among durables to make the most of what we have. But how do we decide between a cheap, used gas guzzler and a more expensive but new fuel-efficient model? Or how do we choose between earning a degree, with no income while we are earning it, and the alternative of continuing to earn today, but with little prospect for career advancement? The economist thinks of the spending of money on automobiles, and of money and time on education, as durable expenditures, and has developed a special approach for making these durable decisions. Central to this approach is a technique for putting all benefits and costs that are incurred in the future into today's values.

We all realize that an offer of a dollar today is better than an ironclad offer of a dollar next year. This is because if we take the dollar today we could put it in a bank, and turn it into more than a dollar next year. If the interest rate were 10 percent, we could turn a dollar today into $1.10 by next year. But if this is so, would you be able to choose between taking a dollar today or $1.10 next year? The answer is that if the 10 percent interest rate is appropriate, you should be indifferent between today's offer of a dollar and a promise of $1.10 due next year.

It is this line of reasoning that allows the economist to put all future costs and benefits into equivalent immediate or *present values*. The present value of $1.10 next year with a 10 percent interest, or *discount rate*, is $1.00. The present value of a dollar next year is therefore $1.00 ÷ 1.10, or approximately $.91. But can we extend this even further ahead?

If you received one dollar today and invested it for two years at 10 percent per year, after the first year it would become $1.10, and on this you will earn 10 percent during the second year. Therefore, after two years your dollar becomes $1.10 × 1.10, or $1.21. The reason why two years interest at 10 percent per year is $.21 and not just $.20 is that you earn interest on your interest, that is, you earn compound interest. But what is the upshot of this for thinking about costs and benefits from durables? It is that $1.21 in two years time when interest rates are 10 percent per annum is worth $1.00 today, and therefore each dollar of benefits or costs in two years is worth $1.00 ÷ 1.21 = $.8264 today.

The calculation of present values from future values follows the general rule of dividing by the amount each original dollar would have become via investing it at compound interest. Because $1.00 invested today for ten years will produce $2.5937 at the end of this time, then $1.00 in ten years is worth only $1.00 ÷ 2.5937 = $.3855 today. Every future value, be it a benefit from what we do or a cost, can be put in present value terms. The burden of the calculation of the present values of costs and benefits is eased by using numerical tables or an electronic calculator with a present value routine. With values for costs and benefits the economist is able to make choices between durables.

Let us go back to the question of which car to buy and let us assume you are choosing between two alternatives, an old clunker costing $2,000 that burns gallons of gas and requires steady maintenance, and a new reliable $6,000 import with a very high fuel-efficiency rating. How would you make the decision given that you could, with sacrifice and perhaps some help, afford either?

The non-economist might be tempted to say that if you can afford the new car that's what you should buy. The economist knows that if you buy the new car you must go without something else, including perhaps eating out or going to the movies every week, so a proper calculation is necessary. This must involve the utility or benefit you get per dollar of cost from the two cars and any alternative purchases, but where the utilities and costs of the cars are spread over time. Let us therefore examine the utilities (or benefits) and costs and see how much they are worth. From what we have said about present values, the further ahead the benefits or costs are, the smaller their importance.

Concentrating on the two cars, the benefit or utility of both is that they provide transportation. If they are both capable of doing this, then the benefits will be similar. We may well wish to add the benefit of the new car that comes in the form of pride of ownership and fun in driving, but let us suppose you live in an environment where this isn't worth very much; perhaps new cars are more likely targets of theft, or a sign you are rich when you don't want to convey this. Let us consider the benefits as being the same. But how about the costs?

The cost of the new car is much higher immediately,

but the future running costs, because of both improved fuel economy and lower maintenance, are lower. Therefore, what the economist does is bring the future costs into their present value. If the old clunker is expected to cost an extra $1,000 per year to run, the extra costs are worth approximately $910 for the first year (this is the present value of $1,000 at 10 percent interest, assuming it is incurred toward the end of the year), $826 for the following year, $751 for the year after that, $683 for the next year, and so on. If this is about the length of time you expect to own either car, we might think of the extra cost of running the clunker as $(910 + 826 + 751 + 683) = $3,170. This must be compared with the extra cost of the new car. But this is not merely the difference in prices between the two cars.

Both cars are likely to have some value when you sell them. The value of the clunker might be expected to be about $800, but the new car might be expected to fetch $1,800. If these amounts are to be received only after four years, the present values are $546 and $1,221. The net purchase cost of the clunker can therefore be thought of as $2,000 − $546, or $1,454, to compare with a net purchase cost of the new car of $6,000 − $1,221 = $4,779. We can therefore think of the total cost of choosing the clunker as $1,454 net of purchase cost, plus $3,170 extra running costs. This is a total of $4,624. This is slightly lower than the cost of the new car net of resale value of $4,779, making the benefit per dollar of the old clunker higher than the benefit per dollar from the new car.

Another way of thinking about the choice between the two cars is to think of the $3,170 lower operating cost of the new car as a benefit of buying it. This benefit might be thought of as having a cost, however, given by the new car's extra cost. Since the purchase prices, net of resale values, are $4,771 versus $1,454, the extra cost of the new car is $3,327. The "benefit" of buying the new car, which is $3,170, is therefore smaller than the cost, so it is not a good idea. Generally, cost savings should be treated as lowering costs rather than as providing benefits; therefore our previous way of thinking, where the benefits are transportation services that are assumed to be the same for both cars, is more appropriate.

The type of thinking we have described should be used for all potential ways of spending or saving income, whether this involves durables like cars, investments in the stock market, or in our own education. We should buy or invest in those opportunities with the highest utility per dollar. When we already own a product such as a car, we need merely think of its "price" as what we would receive by selling it, because this is what we "pay" by not selling it, that is, its opportunity cost. Consequently, in our example of choosing a car, there is no change if we already own an old clunker we could sell for $2,000, and we are deciding whether to replace it with a new car. The calculation is just as before.

In the foregoing example the benefits, in the form of transportation services, were the same whatever our choice. If we turn to the economist's way of thinking about investing in an education we can show an application of benefit-cost analysis where our decision affects both benefits and costs.

Suppose you are currently employed at $25,000 per year. You expect your income to grow by a couple of thousand dollars per year, but the prospects of moving ahead rapidly are limited. You have looked into going to business school for a Master of Business Administration degree (M.B.A.), and tuition plus books are $6,000 per year for each of the two years it will take to earn the degree. Because you will have to be away, the estimated cost of board and other incidentals is $12,000 per year, which is about what you currently spend on rent, food, and so on. Finally, let us suppose you have learned that with the M.B.A. from the good business school you are considering, you can expect to start working at a salary that should be at least $5,000 per year higher than what you would be earning if you stayed in your current job.

The non-economist is likely to reason like this: "The cost of the two-year M.B.A. is $12,000 for tuition, plus $24,000 living expenses. The benefits are at least $5,000 per year for, let us say, forty years. The cost is therefore $36,000 and the benefit at least $200,000. There is little doubt that the M.B.A. is a good idea." Even if the non-economist puts the extra income in present value terms, it still looks like the M.B.A. pays.

The economist thinks very differently. To begin with, the cost of the M.B.A. is not $12,000 tuition plus $24,000 living expenses. The tuition is actually $6,000, plus the present value of $6,000 in a year's time, the latter being worth $5,455 if we stick with a 10 percent discount rate. Therefore, the present value of tuition is $11,455. But what about the living expenses? The economist reasons that living expenses are incurred whether you go to business school or not. They do not, therefore, represent a cost of going for the M.B.A. and should not be included in the calculation of the cost.

This does not mean that the economist considers the total cost of the M.B.A. as $11,455—far from it. The economist recognizes another important cost of being in school. This is the opportunity cost resulting from leaving your job. By being at school you give up $25,000 in the initial year and an estimated $27,000 in the second year. This is definitely a cost of getting a degree, because if you didn't go to school it wouldn't be borne.

The economist reasons that the costs to which we should compare the benefits of an M.B.A. are $11,545 for tuition, plus the opportunity cost of foregone income. The latter is $25,000 plus the present value of $27,000 which is $24,545, providing an opportunity cost of $49,545. When added to the tuition, the total present value of costs of getting the degree is $61,090. This is a lot larger than the cost that most non-economists would associate with the degree.

The economist might also be tempted to add a cost of having to work harder as a student than as an employee in the previous job. But since there could well be some satisfaction connected with learning, which the economist refers to as a *non-pecuniary* or *psychic* benefit, we can suppose this all washes out. But what is the value of the M.B.A. to which we should compare the cost of $61,090?

If the extra income we expect from the M.B.A. is a steady $5,000, we can say that the benefit is the present value of a steady $5,000 per year for, say, forty years. However, as you must wait two years for this, the value is a little lower than $5,000 extra per year starting immediately. For this calculation the economist can look at a present value table or make a quick calculation. The present value of $5,000 per year for forty years starting in two years time and discounted at 10 percent is $40,410. If this seems rather small, recall that as we look at the value of amounts further and further into the future these values fall off quickly, and that

$5,000 per year projected well into the future, has very little present value.

An economist finds a cost of about $60,000 and a benefit of $40,000 for an M.B.A. What looked like a sure bet to the non-economist is a bad proposition to the economist. The reason for the dramatic difference is primarily that the non-economist underestimated the cost by excluding the foregone income of the current job, and overestimated the benefit by not putting the extra income in terms of present values. To a limited extent the erroneous inclusion of living costs offset the errors, but not by a sufficient amount to make the two conclusions agree.

The economist is able to take the calculation further and explain some important observations that appear reasonable to non-economists only in retrospect. Consider the effect of being currently unemployed on the chance that you will attend business school. The non-economist is likely to reason that if you have no income from which to save, this should reduce the chance you will go for the degree. The economist recognizes that you can sometimes borrow against your expected future income. You can therefore attend school if it is a good proposition and we can redo our calculation.

If you are currently unemployed, the total cost of the M.B.A. is substantially reduced. If we use the figures we just cited we find the only relevant cost of the M.B.A. is the tuition, which has a present value of only $11,545. This is the total cost if you expect to be out of work for two years. Even if you thought that by looking for two years you would have found work so that the extra income from the M.B.A. is still only $5,000 per year, rather than the full income you would be receiving with the degree, the decision is still very straightforward. The benefit of about $40,000 vastly exceeds the $11,545 cost. Because others will be influenced just like you from being unemployed, we can expect the number of applications to attend business or law school to increase during times of heavy unemployment, and this is confirmed by the data.

The calculation of the benefits and costs of an undergraduate degree is just a straightforward extension of what we have done for the M.B.A. However, when we consider an undergraduate degree it becomes clear that psychic or non-pecuniary benefits must be included. Even if the degree is not financially worthwhile, it is an investment in the broadening of your horizons into the pleasures of art, literature, travel, the environment, and so on, and society in general is benefited from a better-educated population. Some economists might try to attach dollar amounts to these types of benefits, but this is very difficult. A basic education, even up to college level, might be considered worthwhile regardless of any purely financial cost-benefit calculation, which is why education is often subsidized with tuition costs well below actual costs, university scholarships, fellowships, student loans, and so forth.

Another implication of the economist's way of making decisions with long-term benefits and/or costs involves the effect of interest rates. We can illustrate the importance of interest rates both in our example involving the choice of cars and in considering whether to get an M.B.A.

Suppose that with everything else unchanged, that is, *ceteris paribus,* there is a sudden drop in interest rates from 10 to 5 percent. Returning to the question of which car we should purchase we find that the present value of the saving of $1,000 per year from the new car will increase from

$3,170 to $3,546, with this consisting of $(952 + 907 + 864 + 823)$. At the same time, the $800 resale value of the old car has a present value of $658 and the $1,800 resale value of the new car has a present value of $1,481. The net of resale cost of the new car is therefore $4,519, or $(6,000 − 1,481)$, while that of the old car is $1,342 or $(2,000 − 658)$. The new car hence costs an extra $3,177 or $(4,519 − 1,342)$, while it lowers running costs by $3,546. Therefore, the lower interest rate makes the saving in operating costs exceed the extra purchase cost, making the new car a worthwhile investment. Because other people are also likely to be finding the purchase of a new car to be worthwhile we can expect the demand for cars to be higher at lower interest rates.

The conclusion that a reduction in the interest rate increases the demand for new cars should come as little surprise to most non-economists. However, the non-economist tends to think of this coming about as a result of the effect of lower interest rates on our monthly payments, with lower payments making a new car more affordable. The economist's conclusion was reached without reference to monthly payments and came about because future benefits from a newer car in terms of fuel efficiency and lower maintenance are worth more when interest rates are lower (each dollar next year is worth $1.00 \div 1.1 = \$.91$ today at a 10 percent interest rate, and $1.00 \div 1.05 = \$.95$ at a 5 percent interest rate). In addition, the depreciation of the new car is reduced relative to that of the clunker because the lower interest rate increases today's value of the new car's higher future resale value.

Looking at the effect of a lower interest rate on the return from getting an M.B.A., the effects are as follows: Tuition becomes $6,000 for the first year plus $5,714 for the second year; the opportunity cost of foregone income is $25,000 for the first year and $25,714 for the second year; therefore the total cost of the degree is $62,428. While this is greater than the cost calculated with an interest rate of 10 percent, the present value of the extra income from the M.B.A. is increased by far more. The extra $5,000 per year for forty years starting at the completion of the degree has a present value of $77,800. This exceeds the cost of the degree making it a good investment; a lower interest rate has completely tipped the scales. How many non-economists would believe that a decrease in interest rates would have such a dramatic effect on the incentive to invest in our own education?

The interest rate is not the only factor that affects the demand for such durables as education and cars. As in the case of nondurable items, changes in the price of a product change the quantity demanded. If the price of the new car were to increase to $6,500, even with the interest rate of 5 percent and everything else unchanged the advantage of the new car, which previously cost $3,177 extra but saved $3,546, is wiped out; the extra $500 on the sticker price exceeds the previous advantage. We find that for the situation we have examined the higher price would eliminate the demand for the new car.

When we consider the market in general, an increase in the price of new cars will not make everyone decide against buying one. For those with a cost saving of more than the assumed $1,000 per year from the new car, a higher price will not make the difference. For example, those who drive a great number of miles and hence save more than $1,000 per year will not be turned off by the higher price. However, the higher the price of new cars the fewer consumers who will find it worthwhile to buy and the lower the quantity demanded will be. This is the conclusion we reached with nondurables.

We can apply the economic way of thinking about decisions involving durables to any number of other household products—personal computers, refrigerators, washing machines, furniture, and so on. However, let us apply it to a decision concerning the house itself.

Suppose you are trying to decide whether to buy or rent a house, and for the sake of keeping the example straightforward, that it is the same house you could either buy or rent. Suppose also that the bank has told you that you can borrow 75 percent of the cost; including your property taxes, monthly payments are $800. Suppose the rent on the same house is also $800, and because you live in a well-managed country it should remain at that price indefinitely. How should you consider whether to buy or rent?

Because the monthly payments are the same whether you choose to buy or rent, the non-economist is likely to say that it is obvious you should buy. After all, at the end of your mortgage you will own the house if you buy it.

The economist would argue that the present value of the house you will eventually own if you choose to buy is lower than its market value will be when it becomes yours. The economist would compute the present value that, because we are looking far into the future, may not be substantial. The next step in the economist's thinking is to include the opportunity cost of your down payment. By assumption, this is 25 percent of the cost of the house; you would still have this to invest and earn interest if you were to rent. The number of dollars you put down today, which is a cost of buying—an opportunity cost—should be compared to the present value of the house you would own after the mortgage is paid if you decided to buy. If the present value of the house is smaller than your down payment you should rent.

We have made this example particularly simple; in reality the benefits of buying should include the pride and extra security of ownership, the benefit of inflation in the value of the house and in the rent you would otherwise pay, and so forth. However, this basic way of thinking can handle all of these complications; while the conclusion might well be different the method of thinking would be the same.

Another interesting instance of thinking economically about durable expenditures—or investments—is the way an economist might think about whether to have another child. You may well have heard that it costs about $150,000 to bring a child up to the point of completing college, and that this has probably lowered birthrates. Frequently, the cost estimates are obtained by merely adding up the costs of taking care of the child—extra food, clothes, health insurance, college tuition—net of tax savings and other benefits. There is no attempt to put costs on a present value basis. In addition, a number of relevant costs are omitted.

The economist might compute the cost of having a child by taking the present value of the monetary layouts for all those items we have listed. However, because such expenditures as those on college are far in the future when the original decision on childbearing is made, those expenditures do not figure in a major way.

Where the economist does find a high cost is often where the non-economist has not looked for it. If the mother decides to stay at home for, say, five years, the present value of the five years of foregone income—which is an opportunity cost—should be included. If an extra child necessitates moving into a larger home the cost of this should also be added. Of course, figured against these costs are some potential benefits of the larger home and even of the change in life-style, so only the costs, net of these benefits, are relevant. But what about the benefits of having a child in terms of the joy and love it can bring?

It is here that the economist admits that economics can provide only part of the answer. Some benefits are just not suited to being calculated. However, in place of making the calculations the economist gains mileage by making the following observation. If people have chosen to have a child, then the benefits must be considered to exceed the cost. Since we can calculate most of the costs, then we know that the benefits are perceived to be at least as large.

What the economist has done is argue that by *revealing their preferences* in choosing to have a child, parents have implicitly put a lower limit on the benefits. In this way the economist can still draw conclusions even when calculations cannot be made.

It should be becoming clear now that there are limitations on thinking economically about some investments. The benefits and costs of having a child are not all calculable. And even if they were, how many people sit down to make the calculation or even act "as if" they do? Even if "incorrect" decisions are made, they do not generally affect the love of the child or more generally, survival. The same is true of buying a house, a new car, an old car, or earning an M.B.A. While the economic way of thinking does provide a method of making these decisions, it is just as well that they are usually made without thinking economically.

Where benefit-cost analysis does come into its own is in

decision making by government and business. Should the government build a new road or school? Should it develop a new bomb or fighter plane? Should a business expand a factory? Should it write a new computer program or buy a new machine? These are all decisions involving benefits and costs, and we should consider how the economist might go about making them.

Suppose the government is deciding whether to build a new freeway around a major city to avoid traffic congestion. The costs are those of construction and dislocation while the construction is underway. However, the government must be careful in the computation of construction costs. What matters is the opportunity cost of the nation's resources that are used in road building. Most often these are reflected in the prices of resources. This is because what the government must pay for cement, steel, and so on is at least what someone else would have paid. And what someone else would have paid is at least what the resources are worth in the private sector. In other words, the government must pay the opportunity cost of the resources to the economy. Yet this is not always the case.

If the people hired to build the road would otherwise have remained unemployed, their wages exceed the opportunity cost of their labor. The government should proceed with the road provided the benefits exceed the opportunity cost, so if it employs the unemployed, their wages should be excluded from the calculation of the construction costs.

But what of the benefits? The benefits of a better road involve the value of the time saved by the drivers who use it. They also include any saving in gasoline by lowering the waste of gas in traffic jams. Other benefits may include a potential reduction in accidents if the new road is safer than the old. Benefits may also be enjoyed from getting pollution out of the town where people live, including air pollution from the gasoline and noise pollution. All of these benefits, and more, must be put into present value terms. They must then be compared to the present value of the costs. If the calculation shows the benefits exceed the costs, then the road is a good idea. However, if there are other investment projects the government is considering the various calculations of the differences between benefits and costs—that is, the *net present values*—should be compared. When not all projects can be afforded only the best that can be afforded should be selected.

Business benefit and cost analysis involves more direct market-observed values. The cost of extending a factory can be estimated. So can the benefit of sales from the extra production the factory allows. As before, if the present value of benefits exceeds the value of costs, the project has a positive net present value and is worthwhile. If there are other projects that compete for the limited funds that are available only those with the highest net present values should be chosen.

The fact that businesses and individuals must choose between alternative projects and purchases is self-evident, certainly when funds are limited. However, when it comes to the government we frequently hear comments which imply that a choice is not always necessary. We hear that the community needs a new hospital or a new fire-hall; the high-school needs a new wing; the sewage lines need replacing; the air force needs a new bomber fleet; and so on. The way the needs are stated there is scarcely an indication that choices must be made. Perhaps this is because people view the government as having no limit on its funds.

THINKING SMALL

While the government can borrow, even it must make choices, sometimes forgoing worthy projects. It is even more important to recognize this need for choice than to know how the choices should be made.

CHAPTER 5

Thinking Efficiently

How to Evaluate
Stocks and Bonds

It doesn't matter if you're rich or poor, as long as
you've got money.   JOE E. LEWIS

I do not believe in the collective wisdom of individual
ignorance.   THOMAS CARLYLE

THE ECONOMISTS' way of thinking about such personal
matters as whether to invest in a new automobile or a
graduate degree is, as we have indicated, a special part of
their thinking on investment. Not surprisingly, the larger
part of that thinking has involved investments in stocks
and bonds.

Non-economists might be tempted to argue that a good
stock for investing our wealth would be that of a company
with strong growth. They might then therefore examine
the past history of the size of different companies, measured
by annual sales or the number of employees, and look for
those companies with steep growth charts. Alternatively,
they might examine the histories of different companies'
stock prices. Those that have climbed rapidly might be

believed to offer good investment prospects. This way of
thinking is certainly very common with stockbrokers who
have little training in economics. Sometimes the history
of the stock price is looked at for more than just the rate
of increase during the past to include the volume of stocks
that have changed hands and whether there are discernible
patterns in the number of stocks traded per day. But it is
past data that are examined whatever the form the chart
gazing takes.

Economists do not think that companies with the fastest
growth rates of sales or number of employees make the
best investments in the stock market. Moreover, they do
not think that the past history of the company's stock
price, or any other generally known matter about the
company, provides any valuable information for deciding
which stocks to invest in.

When we buy a stock we might think of the share of
the capital equipment, inventory, land, goodwill, and so
forth it represents. That is, we might think in terms of the
share of the company's *equity* we have purchased. Alternatively, we can think of the share of the company's profits
that the stock gives us the right to receive. The economist
believes that the second viewpoint is more useful. Having
the most fantastic machinery, inventory, and other assets
is of little use if the company cannot make a profit and
cannot pay dividends.

Because future dividends are not known at the time of
buying a stock, it is expected future dividends that determine stock values. Moreover, as with the evaluations of
graduate degrees and new cars, the expected future dividends must be put in terms of present values. The economist thinks of the value of a stock as the present value of

expected future dividends it provides to its owner. However, the present value must be calculated very carefully.

When we described the calculation of present values for the evaluation of a new car or a degree, we merely used the term, "the" interest rate. For example, we said that if we could earn 10 percent per annum then $1 saved today would provide $1.10 next year, so $1.10 next year is worth $1 today. But where do we get the 10 percent from? In particular, how do we choose from among the many rates of interest that are quoted on bank deposits, savings and loan company deposits, municipal bonds, long-term government bonds, treasury bills, and so on?

What we must recognize is that when we use interest rates to compute the present value of the fuel savings from a new car, we are viewing the investment of funds on which we would otherwise have earned interest as an alternative to spending them on the car. Obviously, it makes sense to use an interest rate on an investment that is no riskier than the return in savings of fuel offered by the new car.

When we evaluated the saving coming via the lower cost of running a newer, fuel-efficient car, we thought of this return in savings of fuel and lower maintenance costs as being certain. In fact, as with returns from stocks this is only an expected return that we do not know with absolute certainty. However, in the case of the cost saving from the car (but probably not with the M.B.A.) it is appropriate to assume that the return is reasonably certain. It is true that the price of gas and servicing could go up or down, and could affect the actual saving from the new car, but other than this the expected cost saving is reasonably predictable depending on currently known fuel-efficiency and reliability estimates. Therefore, it is appropriate when evaluating the saving from a car to use an interest rate—or a discount rate—which is what we could get on our savings if they were not at risk.

However, the return on a stock is very uncertain. Actual dividends may differ substantially from our expectations, and as a result the stock price itself can go up or down dramatically. Therefore, when we compute the present value of expected dividends generated by the stock, we must be careful to use an interest rate for an alternative investment to the stock that has the same risk characteristic as the stock. This might be the interest rate on low-grade corporate bonds or on uninsured second mortgages. Because the riskier alternative investments generally offer a higher expected return to compensate for their extra risk, the discount rate will exceed the discount rate we might use to evaluate a new car. The greater the risk of the stock the higher the rate at which we should discount expected future dividends.

After we have settled on a discount rate and have taken the expected present value of the dividends, if we discover that the value of the stock we obtain is higher than the price of the stock on the stock market, the stock is a good investment. However, it is extremely unlikely that we will find stocks that have a price below their present value to us.

The market price of a stock reflects what people expect the dividends to be, with these discounted at an interest rate they believe to reflect the risk. It follows that we will come up with a greater value than the price we must pay only if we expect the dividends to be higher than others do, or if we think the discount rate that reflects risk is lower than that used by other people. This immediately suggests asking how we make our estimate of the future dividends and how other people, who collectively constitute the market, form their expectations. It also suggests asking how we and the market in general come up with the discount rate. In turn, the latter question involves the calculation of the risk we and others associate with the stock.

On the question of dividends, what most people do in forming an estimate of what these are likely to be is to begin by looking at what these have been in the past, including the growth rate. The higher dividends have been and the faster these have been growing, the higher dividends are likely to be in the future.

Unless we have what economists refer to as *insider information,* which is considered illegal by the police department of the stock market, the Securities and Exchange Commission, the information we have to go on is the same information available to everyone else. This includes the history of dividends and any special news about the company in terms of takeover bids for it or bids it has made, and so forth. Because other participants in the market know what we do, they are likely to form the same expectations of future dividends as we are. It follows that provided we use the same discount rate as others, the value of the stock to us will be the same as its value to others, which in turn is the price of the stock in the marketplace. There are therefore no bargain stocks because if any company has particularly good prospects for dividends this will become known to others and will be reflected in the market price of the company's stock.

The fact that market prices reflect all the publicly available information on a company's prospects is referred to by economists as *market efficiency*. Market efficiency means that provided the discount rate we and others use for calculating present values are the same, the value of a stock to us is the same as its market.price—unless we have insider information.

The obvious question to ask next is will the discount rate we use for computing the present values of expected dividends be the same rate that others are using? The economist will answer that it is.

As we have already mentioned, the economist thinks that the riskier an investment the higher its expected return must be. This higher expected return merely compensates for the risk. Of course, since there is risk, the actual return we receive is not known in advance. For this reason, by expected return we do not mean a specific value that is held with certainty, but rather the average of a number of potential outcomes. Each of the potential outcomes would be included within the average according to how likely that outcome is. (Those with a knowledge of statistics will recognize the expectation as the *mean* of potential outcomes.)

Since the market, like ourselves, is likely to use a higher discount rate for expected dividends the riskier these dividends are, we will value a stock at above its market price because of the discount rate only if we perceive the stock to be safer than others do. But is this likely to happen?

Economists think of the risk of a stock in terms of the extent to which its price might go up or down, and because the price reflects expected dividends the risk ultimately depends on how much the dividends might vary. The more volatile the performance the higher the risk. But according to economic thinking, it is not the volatility of the stock itself that matters. This is because the economist knows that people do not hold an individual stock in isolation, but rather hold it within a "portfolio" containing numerous stocks. The risk that any individual stock therefore provides is not the risk of that stock itself, but the risk it contributes to an efficiently selected portfolio.

When we own a large number of stocks we can expect to benefit from not having all our eggs in the same basket, which economists refer to as the benefit of a *diversified portfolio*. If we add another stock to this already diversified portfolio, it will not make that portfolio riskier by the amount of risk of the added stock. This is not obvious, and can take a moment of reflection before it is clear. (Nobody said that everything the economist thinks is straightforward. If this were so, economists would not be able to make a living explaining how they think.)

Not all stocks go up and down in price at the same time, and they certainly don't go up and down by the same amount. This means that if we held a number of stocks, while some stocks are doing poorly others may be doing well, and even if they are also doing poorly they may not be as badly off as others. Consequently, if we examined the total market value of a portfolio of stocks this is not likely to be as volatile as the sum of the volatilities of the individual stocks within the portfolio. (Volatility is judged by a statistical measure of dispersion called *variance* or *standard deviation,* but this need not concern us here.) Therefore, what is the risk we should attach to any individual stock in a diversified portfolio for determining an appropriate discount rate? The answer is that it is the extent to which that particular stock increases the risk of the portfolio, which because the portfolio offers risk diversification is smaller than the risk of the stock when judged in isolation.

Because the market in general can, like ourselves, reduce the riskiness of an individual stock by adding it to a portfolio, the discount rate the market will use will be smaller than that warranted by the riskiness of the stock itself. The market therefore uses a rather low discount rate for computing present values. This makes the market price of the stock relatively high. Only if we can combine the stock within as diversified a portfolio as others in the market are we likely to come up with as high a value of the stock as the market price.

You might be surprised that all the economist needs in order to value a stock are the expected dividends and an interest rate reflecting the risk the stock contributes to a portfolio. What about the value of the stock at the end, when we sell it? Didn't we need the resale values to make the choice between a new and an old car? Therefore, don't we need the expected value of the stock when we sell it?

The economist reasons that the value of a stock when we sell it reflects the expected future dividends at that time, put into their present value at an appropriate interest rate for the risk the stock contributes to a diversified market portfolio. It follows that the value of the stock is still determined only by the dividends and discount rate. Some dividends we will receive and others the buyer receives, but because the buyer pays us the value of these dividends, from our perspective the value of the stock is the present value of all the expected future dividends for as long as the company is in operation. Indeed, because our expectations and those of others in the market are based on the same public information, the price of the stock when we sell it is the value of those same dividends to us. Therefore, we can think of the value of a stock as the present value of just the dividends, with this taking care of the price of the stock when we sell it.

You might have been concerned not only with the role of the selling price of the stock, but with the problem of a company retaining earnings rather than distributing them to shareholders. In particular, could it be that by retaining some of the profits dividends are reduced and the value of the stock is then adversely affected?

The economist has an intriguing way of thinking about the question of retained versus distributed earnings. Apart from complications introduced by taxes, the economist thinks that it does not matter whether a company keeps and reinvests everything it earns or pays it all out as dividends to shareholders.

The economist reasons that if earnings are retained and reinvested current dividends are reduced, but future dividends are increased by the returns on the reinvested earnings. If the return earned by the company is the same as that available to shareholders, every $1.00 reinvested will generate future dividends with a present value to shareholders of $1.00. For example, if $1.00 retained and invested by the firm yields 12 percent, then at year's end the firm will receive $1.12. If shareholders are using a 12 percent interest rate to compute present values this $1.12 next year will have a present value of $1.00. Hence, if the opportunities open to the firm are about as good as those open to the shareholders, the reinvestment of retained earnings does not cause their present value to change.

The conclusion that in the absence of taxes it doesn't matter whether a firm pays out its profits as dividends or retains and invests them is not what many non-economists would have thought. If individual income taxes are allowed for even fewer non-economists would reach the economist's conclusion.

The retaining of earnings shifts shareholders' returns from dividends, which are taxed as income, to capital gains, which have a lower tax rate. It follows that by retaining earnings a firm increases share values; by lowering taxes shareholders are prepared to pay more for the company's shares. Indeed, if we pursue this line of reasoning it is difficult to explain why dividends are paid at all! Some rather elaborate explanations for paying dividends have been developed including one in which they signal to shareholders that all is well. However, these explanations go a bit beyond the focus of normal economic thinking, which leaves us with the remarkable conclusion that the more profit a company retains the more valuable are its shares.

Another conclusion from thinking economically about stocks is that shareholders cannot be made better off by having *stock splits*. These occur when a company gives its shareholders two or more shares for each share they own. Since stock splits have no effect on future expected total dividends or on the correct interest rate for discounting, they cannot affect share values. All that happens is that each share represents a proportionately smaller claim against total earnings. Of course, if the stock split occurs because share prices have increased in value the shareholder will be richer, but not because of the stock split itself—unless this is taken by the market to indicate improved future prospects.

Perhaps the most striking implication of the economists' way of thinking about stocks is that which follows from their argument that the stock market is efficient. We recall that this means that all the publicly available information about a company is reflected in the company's stock price. If this is true, only new information can move the price of the stock. However, this is as likely to be positive information on the company as it is to be negative. This means that prices of stocks are just as likely to go up as to go down from one day to the next. This is known as a *random walk* and it means that you might as well pick your stocks by randomly sticking a pin into the stock market page of your newspaper as by spending hours doing *fundamental analysis*. After all, what you find out, if it involves only public information, should already be reflected in the stock's price.

Few non-economists, certainly those who sell advice, are likely to believe this implication of efficiency. Surely someone knows better than the market. But what is it they know? If it is what others know, because it is publicly available information such as the record of profitability, pending takeover bids, and so forth, the stock's price will already reflect the information. The prices of stocks of companies with good prospects will have been bid up in the market to the point where the dividends they are expected to provide offer a fair expected return, given the risk of the company's stock within a portfolio. The prices of stocks of companies with poor prospects will as compensation be low so that they too offer a fair return for their risk.

Extensive research on stock price data almost universally indicates that stock markets are efficient. This has been discovered by showing that prices behave randomly from day to day. The only valuable advice is illegal advice available to insiders, and few stocktraders are on the inside. If they are, they are likely to end up eventually really on the inside—behind bars.

After what we have said, it should not be difficult to see

why the economist believes that the size of a company measured in terms of sales or number of employees is not relevant for the value of its stock. Company size is not necessarily related to profits. There are many mammoth companies that lose money and some of these have actually experienced increasing sales. Dividends cannot be paid indefinitely if a company has lots of red ink, so it is dividends or profits, and not the size of the company that is relevant.

When we turn to the determination of bond prices, the relevant factors have nothing to do with dividends, but rather concern interest rates. Indeed, economic thinking must start from the basic relation between the value of bonds and interest rates.

Unlike stocks that are never redeemed and pay dividends not known in advance, bonds repay their principal at *maturity* and generally pay *coupons* which are fixed. A bond might offer $100 per year at year's end for the next twenty years, with $1,000 of principal repaid at the end of the twentieth year. Therefore, in order to determine how much this bond is worth it is necessary to value the $100 per year at an appropriate discount rate. Since the appropriate discount rate is the opportunity cost we face, it is reasonable to use the market interest rate we would earn today on a new bond. If a new bond offers 10 percent interest, the value of an old, or *seasoned,* bond is the present value of $100 per year for twenty years, with $1,000 redemption value in the twentieth year. It turns out that at a 10 percent interest or discount rate, the seasoned bond is worth exactly $1,000.

You might be surprised that $100 per year for twenty years plus $1,000 at the end of twenty years is worth only $1,000. The reason is that if the going interest rate is 10 percent we could take $1,000 today and invest it to earn

$100 each year, and still have our $1,000 of principal at the end. Therefore, we would be indifferent between buying a seasoned bond offering coupons of $100 on $1,000, and investing in a new bond that offers a 10 percent interest rate. But what if the interest rate on new bonds were to change from 10 percent? How much could we sell our $100 coupon bond for if new bonds came out offering 12 percent?

When interest rates increase to 12 percent we can take $1,000 and earn $120 per annum, still getting back our $1,000 principal at the maturity of the bond. Consequently, if we hold a bond offering only $100 per annum, it will not be worth a full $1,000. The value it will have is such that the $100 coupons and $1,000 back at the end represent a 12 percent yield, the opportunity cost to the buyer. This value is approximately $850. Nobody would pay more than this amount for our $100 coupon bond because at a 12 percent discount rate the present value of the $100 per year and $1,000 at the end is this amount. Alternatively, at a bond price of $850, the $100 coupons give a rate of return of approximately 12 percent, the same as that offered on new bonds.

If instead of increasing, interest rates had declined, our bond offering $100 per annum would have increased in value. For example, if interest rates fell from 10 percent to 8 percent, $100 per year with $1,000 at the end of twenty years has a present value of approximately $1,200.

Because of the direct link between bond prices and interest rates economists are able to think of the reason bond prices change purely in terms of the reasons for changes in interest rates. This leads them into macroeconomics and an examination of such factors as inflation, government deficits, and so on.

We have no reason to delve into the forces behind interest rates to contrast economic thinking with that of non-economists. It is not uncommon to hear those without economic training talking of interest rates as if they were set by the banks. Higher rates are seen as the result of bankers setting out to increase profits. What is frequently overlooked is that when market forces drive up interest rates, banks and other lenders are forced to pay more as well as charge higher rates. They are merely the agents that get the brunt of the public's attention, but who are themselves responding to the market.

Interest rates, and hence bond prices, have important effects on the stock market because stocks and bonds are substitutes in the sense that to savers they represent two different ways of holding wealth. When interest rates on bonds increase, that is, when bond prices decline, the dividends on stocks do not look as good compared to the higher yields on bonds. Therefore, in order for stocks to offer competitive yields it is necessary for their prices to decline. At the lower stock prices, the expected future dividends represent a higher expected return. Hence, declines in bond prices—that is, increases in interest rates—cause declines in stock prices.

There is another way of viewing the effect of interest rates on stock prices. Recall that the price of a stock is the present value of the expected dividends. The present value is calculated by finding the amount needed today to provide each dollar in the future at the given interest rate. The higher the interest rate, the lower the present value will be. Hence, the higher interest rates are the lower stock prices will be for given expected future dividends.

You might now well be wondering whether there are any benefits to be derived from thinking economically about stocks and bonds. The answer is that apart from appreciating what is happening, there are no rewards from applying economic thinking to the stock and bond markets. Market efficiency means that fabulous returns have been removed by the many others who would also like to get rich. Even the economist is left facing only "normal" expected returns. This is confirmed by the fact that most economists, even those who think remarkably well, are salaried employees of universities and governments.

CHAPTER 6

Thinking Productively

How Firms Set
Output Levels

Monopoly is business at the end of its journey.
HENRY DEMAREST LLOYD

Without competition there are no winners.
Anonymous

WE HAVE SEEN how the economist thinks about demand, whether it be for a new car or the stock of a car company. Now it is time to think about the factors that affect supply and how the economist's thinking differs from that of non-economists.

Sometimes we hear people talking as if supply were of a fixed or given amount. We might hear that old master paintings or urban land make good investments because their supply cannot be increased. At other times it sounds as if it is demand that is of a given amount, and that producers are happy to supply whatever amount happens to be demanded. For example, bakers or automobile producers might argue that they make an amount each month or week that they think they can sell, and that they would make more if they could sell more; "we supply our customers' demands" might be their claim. These views represent the extreme situations of the economist's theory of supply.

According to the economist the quantity of a product that is supplied is, in general, neither fixed nor completely flexible, but depends on, among other things, a product's price. The degree of response could vary between no response when the supply is fixed, and accommodation of any level of demand when production conditions are flexible. However, the response of the quantity supplied to a product's price is between these levels, with technological conditions and the amount of time allowed for adjustment determining the actual degree of response. As with demand, economists do not always begin by directly making assumptions about how the quantity varies with a product's price, but rather derive this from other more basic assumptions. Perhaps the most basic assumption in the economist's thinking on supply is that firms choose their production in order to maximize their profits.

In some political camps profit is little more than a six-letter word that conjures up an image of all the bad in capitalist society. The economist thinks of profit as a powerful motivator and defines it as the excess of what firms take in as revenues, and what they pay out as costs.

There are different accounting conventions for treating interest expenses, depreciation, and so on, that can cloud the measurement of costs. Even revenues are not clear-cut when credits are granted. However, many economists never study accounting, so their theory is not dependent on accounting measures. Indeed, the concepts used in the economist's theory of supply are not directly available in any financial accounting statements.

A company's revenues are its receipts from customers, and they increase with the amount the company sells and the prices of its products. Costs are incurred in the payment for raw materials, wages, utilities, rent, interest, certain taxes, and so on. By varying output, firms can change both their revenues and their costs. Economists assume they do this until the difference between total revenues and costs—profits—are at a maximum.

The economist's assumption that firms select their output to maximize profits is the counterpart of the assumption that consumers select what they buy to maximize their utility. This reveals a great similarity in basic structure between the theory of supply and the theory of demand. Both establish what it is that motivates people—the consumers or the firms. Both are assumed to be maximizing certain objectives. Then both theories establish what it is that constrains people—income for consumers and the costs of production for producers. This is a standard pattern found in the mathematics of maximization subject to constraints, namely an *objective function* and a statement of the *constraints* to be satisfied. Indeed, the dual assumptions used in the theories of supply and demand make them immediately amenable to mathematics. However, the most important conclusions do not require mathematics and can be reached by the power of thinking.

It follows immediately from defining profits as the excess of revenues over costs that profits are increased from adding to output if this increases revenues more than costs. In the case of a firm that can sell whatever quantity it wants at the going market price, the increase in revenue from selling another unit of output must be the price of the product. Therefore, if the price exceeds the production costs, profits are increased from adding to output. By the economist's assumption that firms maximize their profits, it follows that output will be increased whenever the price exceeds the production costs. Let us apply this to a specific situation and suppose that, perhaps because you earned your M.B.A., you have been put in charge of an automobile plant making a sportscar called "The Sting" and that you have been told that you can sell up to 10,000 of them per month at a price of $10,000 each.

If you had a good course in economics while earning your business degree you would call in the production engineer and get an estimate of costs. Suppose you are told that given the limitations of the fixed factory size and the consequent difficulty of substantially expanding output, at 5,000 cars produced per month, the 5,000th car has a cost of $8,000, and that at 5,500 per month the 5,500th car costs $8,500. Suppose further that the 6,000th car costs $9,000, the 6,500th costs $10,000, the 7,000th, $12,000, and so on. These are the *marginal costs*. By definition, marginal cost is the cost of another unit of output.

It is obvious that by increasing output from 5,000 per month to 5,001 per month you would increase profits. This is because you can sell cars for $10,000 that cost $8,000 to produce, adding $2,000 to your profit for each additional car produced. At 6,000 a month you are still adding to profit by making additional cars since they cost $9,500 and sell for $10,000. At 6,500 produced per month, extra cars cost the same to produce as you receive from selling them. Consequently, it does not pay to produce

7,000 cars per month, for the last 500 cars cost more to manufacture than you would receive for them.

It should be clear from the example that the rule for profit maximization is to find the rate of production where the marginal cost equals the car's price. Below this production level profits are increased by increasing output, and above this level profits are increased by reducing output.

It also should be clear, even without an M.B.A., that if the marginal cost is constant at, for example, $8,000, while the price is constant at $10,000, there would be no limit on the number of cars you should produce; the more cars you make, the more profits you make. Therefore, it is an important part of the economist's thinking on supply to explain why the marginal cost increases, or why the market price decreases, as you add to output.

As we have already indicated, the basis of the increase in marginal cost is a short-run limitation on the size of the factory and the rate of production it can handle. We can see this if we think of a plant that has been built for producing 5,000 units per month and ask what happens if you try to produce more.

Even if the plant has been designed for 5,000 units you could build more by taking certain steps. For example, you could add an extra shift, perhaps at night or on the weekend. However, this involves paying overtime, increasing the cost per car as more are produced—an increase in marginal cost at higher output. Instead of running extra shifts, existing shifts could be beefed up with more people operating the currently available equipment. For example, the production line may be kept going more rapidly during coffee breaks, restroom breaks, and so on. However, extra people on the same machines will not be as productive as those for whom the equipment was intended; if everybody on the line had a job before there are unlikely to be super-productive new jobs.

The assumption that with a fixed plant size marginal costs eventually increase is called the *Law of Diminishing Returns*. Economists are careful to distinguish this Law of Diminishing Returns from *diminishing returns to scale*.

The Law of Diminishing Returns is valid only when a *factor of production,* such as the car factory, is fixed in size. The law then says that the cost of getting an extra unit of output, the marginal cost, will increase after some particular production level. Returns to scale refer to the situation when more of every factor of production—the raw materials, people working, equipment, and so on—can be used to increase output. When more of every factor is used, that is, when the scale of production is increased, then the cost of extra units may increase if there are *decreasing returns to scale.* However, this is no more likely than *increasing returns to scale,* which is when per unit production costs decline with expansion of output.

It is not difficult to provide examples of industries that exhibit increasing returns to scale. In financial services scale allows the use of main-frame computers that reduce costs. In the manufacture of many consumer durables, like televisions and video recorders, costs fall over time as output is expanded. However, in the short run, with fixed numbers of computers or factory sizes, even these industries which enjoy increasing returns to scale face the Law of Diminishing Returns. The law is, therefore, a valid assumption despite the possibility of increasing returns to scale.

The other important assumption in our car example is

that you can sell more and more of The Sting without lowering the price. However, as we saw in chapters 3 and 4, generally more can be sold only by lowering prices. This means that the extra revenue from selling another car is no longer the price received for that car; revenue is lost on other cars because of the need to lower prices to sell the extra car. When the reduced revenue on other cars is included we have the economist's concept of *marginal revenue*. By definition this is the extra revenue from selling an extra car.

To take a specific example to illustrate the concept of marginal revenue, suppose that 6,500 Stings can be sold if the price is $10,000 each, but that to sell an extra car, that is, the 6,501st, the price must be lowered to $9,999. The total revenue when 6,500 Stings are sold at $10,000 is $65,000,000. The total revenue when 6,501 are sold at $9,999 is $65,003,499. We see that the extra total revenue, which we have called the marginal revenue, from selling the 6,001st car is only $3,499. It is only this relatively small amount because while the car itself sells for $9,999, in order to sell it the price of the previously sold 6,500 must be reduced by $1. The net gain, the marginal revenue, is therefore $9,999 − $6,500, or $3,499.

When higher sales can be achieved only by reducing prices, the economist's rule for how much to produce becomes that production should be set where marginal revenue equals marginal cost. The only change from the previous rule is that instead of equating the marginal cost to the price, we equate the marginal cost and the marginal revenue.

The fact that the marginal revenue is often lower than the price is important for explaining why profit maximizing output is limited, even in the long run when The Sting or some other product is subject to increasing returns to scale. In such a case, we reach a point where the revenue of an extra unit is lower than the cost not because marginal costs are increasing, but because marginal revenues are decreasing.

Every firm, whether or not its long run marginal costs decline with output and whether or not it is a monopolist, faces a limit imposed by the market. The basis of this limit is that a firm can expand sales only by lowering prices; it cannot set both the price and quantity. It can set the quantity it produces and let the market determine the price. Alternatively, it can set a price and see how much it can sell at that price. However, it cannot independently set both price and quantity; whatever it sets, extra sales will result in declining marginal revenues.

Let us return to the automobile factory and suppose that there is suddenly an increase in the market price of cars. In particular, let us suppose you are told by the marketing department that because demand is strong, you can sell your current output of The Sting not for $10,000, but for $10,500 each.

If you had been maximizing profits and had chosen an output where the marginal revenue and marginal cost were equal, the higher price would mean you should produce more. This is because the higher price means a higher marginal revenue that will exceed the marginal cost at your current output. However, as you expand output the marginal cost will increase. You should therefore select a new output where the marginal cost has risen to the marginal revenue. The higher price of The Sting suggests you should order an expansion of monthly production.

The conclusion that you should order an increase in production as the price increases was made at the beginning of this chapter. We have just seen why. Moreover, the way we reached the conclusion also reveals what it is that determines how much more you should produce. It should be clear that the more slowly marginal cost increases as output is expanded, the greater the increase in output that should be ordered. In addition, the slower marginal revenues decrease with output the greater the expansion should be. If the extra output starts to force down the price of The Sting to below $10,500, the more the price drops from adding to output, the smaller the output increase you should order. We see that it is production and marketing conditions that determine the response of supply to changes in price.

We might next ask what economic thinking implies if marginal costs increase at every level of output. Let us suppose that auto workers suddenly gain a hike in wages.

If output had been where marginal cost and marginal revenue were equal, higher wages will push marginal cost above marginal revenue. At your current output level "marginal" cars will be costing more than they add to your revenue. Output should therefore be cut back. Similarly, if marginal costs decline marginal cars will become suddenly profitable and you should produce more.

Many non-economists will not find the conclusion that you should reduce production after an increase in the marginal cost, and increase production after a decrease in marginal costs, as too surprising. However, most non-economists when asked what the effect of an increase in production costs would do would probably answer that it would cause an increase in the price of cars. They are likely to think that as costs increase you would add this to the price. The economist reasons that it is the reduction in output or supply that forces prices higher. Therefore, the economist's conclusion is not different from that of the non-economist, but recognizes that prices are determined in the market rather than just set by producers.

Where the conclusions of the economist and the non-economist do differ is on the effect of an increase in production cost that is not a variable cost. Variable costs are those that depend on output. However, there are other costs that are "fixed" and do not depend on the amount produced, at least in the short run. An example would be interest payments on previously incurred debt or property taxes that are the same whether an auto plant is making 500 or 5,000 cars each month. But what does an economist think an increase in fixed costs will do?

Because profit maximization involves finding the output at which marginal costs equal marginal revenues, a change in fixed costs will do nothing to output; it doesn't enter the calculation. Moreover, because the profit-maximizing output is not affected by fixed costs, nor is the price affected. With the same quantity being supplied the market price will also be the same. This is a remarkable conclusion that few, if any, non-economists are likely to reach. We find that while changes in some costs will affect the profit-maximizing prices and output, other costs will have no short-run effect.

While fixed costs have no effect on output or prices in the short run there are effects in the long run when, by definition, firms have a chance to adjust fixed factors. In the long run an increase in fixed costs will reduce profitability because profits are revenues minus costs, including both variable and fixed costs. Lower profitability discourages new firms from entering an industry, and if the increase in fixed costs is substantial it might encourage existing firms to leave the industry. Industry output might therefore eventually decline, forcing up prices. However, it is only when firms have packed up and moved out of the industry that this will happen. Therefore we discover that the view that cost increases are associated with price increases is valid in the short run and in the long run if the costs are variable costs that affect marginal costs. However, this view is valid only in the long run if higher costs are fixed costs.

When fixed costs decline, output is not immediately affected, as in the case of increased fixed costs. However, lower costs with unchanged output, and therefore the same total revenue, mean higher profits. If the industry is open to new firms—a prerequisite for an industry to be *competitive*—the higher profits will attract new producers. This means that profits will not permanently remain above a *normal level,* which by definition is the rate of profit sufficient to keep new firms from entering a particular industry and existing firms from leaving. If profits increase above the normal level, expansion of the industry would eventually lower the market price and restore profit rates to normal.

Free entry not only keeps profits from remaining abnormally high, but also forces firms to produce at the lowest possible cost. This is because new firms join an industry until the market price reaches a level relative to costs at which only a normal profit can be made. If any firm is selling at the same price as other firms—as it must in a competitive market—but operating at higher costs than the others, that firm's profits will be lower than others, that is, below normal. Because by definition the normal level is just sufficient to keep the firm interested in continuing to produce, if profits fall below this level the firm will leave the industry. Only those firms producing at the lowest possible production costs will remain.

For competitive firms, the prices of their products can be taken as given since each individual firm is too small to affect market prices by varying its output. This means that in equalizing marginal costs and marginal revenues the firms are also equalizing marginal costs and prices; extra sales do not involve lower prices on non-marginal units. However, in an industry that is supplied by a firm with monopoly power marginal revenue is lower than the price. This is because in order to sell an extra unit of output a monopoly must reduce its price on all units it sells. The reduced price on all units sold lowers the extra revenue from the extra unit to below the price.

An industry controlled by a monopolist will provide a lower output than competitive firms would collectively provide if the industry were made competitive. This is because for monopolists the marginal revenue is lower than the price. By equating marginal revenue with marginal cost, the monopolist's marginal cost will also be below the price, and therefore lower than would occur in a competitive situation. If costs are determined by technology and prices of inputs, and these are the same whether an industry is competitive or controlled by a monopolist, then a lower marginal cost requires lower output. This follows from the law of diminishing returns.

Because monopolists operate with a lower output they will also be able to sell their product at a higher price than would competitive firms. This is the reason why economists are so fond of competition; it provides more at lower prices.

The conclusion that firms with monopoly power charge more than competitive firms is likely to surprise few non-economists. However, the conclusion that monopolists will not produce as much may surprise them. Since monopolists control the market it might seem that they could force us to buy their output. The reason why monopolists restrain output is the declining demand they would face if they increased their prices. They would rather cut output and save costs and also extract a high price.

Another issue on which the thinking of non-economists differs from that of economists concerns the effect of taxes. Non-economists often talk as if firms increase prices to cover higher taxes, but the economist knows that the effect of taxes is considerably more complicated than this. Indeed, in certain circumstances tax increases have no effect on prices. In the short run, taxes can affect prices and output only if they affect marginal costs or revenues, while in the long run they must affect the entry or exit of firms in an industry. It is only in these ways that taxes can affect the quantity supplied or demanded, and thereby market prices.

Taxes paid by producers on each unit they manufacture work like increases in marginal costs. They reduce the profit-maximizing output because at the original rate of output the marginal cost, including the tax, will exceed marginal revenue. The lower output will force up the price. However, this is not because each firm tacks on the tax to its selling price because each firm must sell at the going price in a competitive industry. Rather, it is because the tax affects each firm's output—which is what they control—and this in turn affects industry output and therefore the market price.

When taxes are the same regardless of output and do not affect marginal cost or revenue they will not affect the profit-maximizing output and therefore will also not affect the price. As we explained before, they are like any other fixed cost. However, in a competitive industry with normal profits before a tax, firms will have subnormal profits after the tax is imposed, and some of these will decide to leave the industry. Output will decline in the long run, forcing higher prices. Firms will continue to leave until the consequent decline in quantity supplied forces up prices to the point of providing normal profits for the remaining firms. Because production costs are not affected by the tax this means that market prices, and therefore the firms' revenues, must eventually increase by the amount of the tax or else profits could not be back to where they were before the tax was imposed.

In a monopolistic environment a tax that does not affect marginal cost or revenue will not affect short-run output just as in a competitive industry. Moreover, provided the tax is not so severe as to put the firm into the red, it will also leave output and market prices unchanged in the long run. Of course, the tax will reduce profits, but as long as they are still considered to provide a sufficient return, given the risk and amount invested, the firm will continue producing. The production level will be the same as the before-tax level because marginal cost and revenue have not changed, and the same output means the same market price. Therefore, fixed taxes are irrelevant for the output and prices of monopolists. Non-economists might have thought that monopolists would be more likely to increase prices to cover taxes than would competitive firms.

This brings us immediately to the question of whether the conclusions we have reached with our fine-tuned thinking are valid. The logic might well be infallible given the assumptions of increasing costs and profit maximization, but do firms really behave as the logic dictates, namely by finding the exact output level where the marginal cost equals the marginal revenue? Indeed, how can firms ever know the marginal cost and marginal revenue that would occur at each possible output? At best, firms are likely to know their total costs and total revenues, and competitive firms in particular might know their marginal revenue because this is the price, but the effect on costs and revenues of an extra unit at every possible output is something else entirely. What is the economist's defense?

To the question of whether firms really do equate marginal cost and marginal revenue economists answer that those firms that survive must behave as if they equate them. If they did not they would be producing inefficiently and would be forced out of business by having subnormal profits. While this argument, based on the principle of survival, does have some basis in the case of firms (unlike the case with consumers) it is a very thin defense. To begin with, it applies only to competitive markets because noncompetitive firms can survive even if they do act inefficiently. But even in a competitive market, if costs do not vary to a great extent with company output—as many studies of production costs have indicated—selecting an output other than the profit-maximizing output may not hurt the firm very much. If marginal costs are relatively constant it doesn't matter what output they produce.

Economists are still left with the defense that the predictions of their theory, such as the effect of changing prices or costs on output, could be qualitatively valid even if the predictions are not quantitatively precise. This is the economist's line of defense used for the theory of demand. However, while many predictions are qualitatively correct, there are predictions that may not be universally accurate. For example, changes in fixed or overhead costs and lump sum taxes, which theoretically should have no effect on output, probably often do affect production and therefore prices.

The validity of the economist's thinking on supply turns out to be at least in part an empirical question, but we can even find potential problems in the assumptions themselves. The assumptions we have used are that in the short run marginal costs eventually increase with increased output, and that firms maximize profits.

We have already mentioned that marginal costs may not increase substantially with expanding output. This is true even in the short run, when firms are constrained by their plant size. Of course, economists cannot relate the short run to any fixed point on a time scale. This makes talk of the "short run" devoid of much practical value. However, the problems stemming from assuming diminishing returns are overshadowed by those stemming from the other assumption, that of profit maximization. There are a number of reasons why objectives may be far more complicated than this.

To begin with, firms are unlikely to attempt to maximize profits in the short run if it conflicts with long-run profit maximization. It may pay to overproduce in the short run or even to give away output in order to attract customers for the future.

Sometimes long-run profit maximization appears in a subtle form. For example, dentists who always seem to be promoting the use of dental floss may well be maximizing long-run profits. While regular flossing tends to reduce the frequency of patient visits in the short run, it also tends to preserve gums and thereby causes people to return for cleaning and checkups of their teeth. People who lose their teeth, who have not flossed, wear plates and do not need to visit ordinary dentists.

THINKING SMALL

In publicly held companies, profit maximization may take the form of maximization of the wealth of shareholders. This provides a maximization of long-run profits because, as we have already seen, share prices reflect both current and expected future profits. However, when we start thinking of who is doing the maximization in publicly held companies we discover a reason why the maximization may involve something other than profits. When there is a separation between the ownership of a firm and its management there is no guarantee that profits will be maximized. The managers are merely the agents of the shareholders and may find a way to maximize their own salaries or prestige by pursuing goals that do not involve maximizing share values. Managers may maximize sales or the number of employees in order to maximize their feelings of self-importance. Alternatively, they might try to surround themselves with attractive staffs, plush carpets, catered lunches, executive jets, or memberships at golf courses rather than spend their time increasing shareholders' profits. The predictions of the tidy theory of production used by the economists are then not valid because managers will not be equalizing marginal costs and marginal revenues.

Rather than strictly equating marginal costs and revenues, managers instead may be following established routines until forced by errors into making changes. They may have what Nobel prize-winning economist Herbert Simon has referred to as *satisficing objectives,* showing concern for complete failure but not worrying too much about producing the precise, "optimum" output. After all, costs and revenues are in reality uncertain and what makes sense in a deterministic environment may not be useful when realizations are uncertain, or *stochastic.* Uncertainty tends to encourage conservative behavior by managers rather than the optimizing behavior which is the basis of the traditional theory; conservative behavior is intelligent if optimization could cause failure. As in the case of preferences in the economist's theory of demand, some of the important questions concerning objectives have been skirted by the economist in avoiding value judgments and taking objectives as given.

Another problem with profit maximization is illustrated by the survival of firms owned by nonmaximizing Quakers. While their beliefs involve values much broader than high profits, they have survived and often have become affluent. This may have to do with the long-run benefits of honesty; they may be attracting some customers because they are known to be honest. However, the traditional theory of supply based on short-run profit maximization cannot capture this. In addition, there are many other providers of goods and services, such as the government and other nonprofit institutions for which the traditional supply theory is not valid.

CHAPTER 7

Balanced Thinking

Equilibrium of Supply and Demand

Talk is cheap because the supply always exceeds the demand. Therefore, people should pay for the privilege of talking and be paid if forced to listen.

Anonymous

The demand exceeds the supply of sex, but only in the case of free love.

Anonymous

IF THERE IS a crowning achievement of economics that has percolated down into everyday thinking it is an appreciation of the law of supply and demand. However, while numerous people without economic training use supply and demand, it is the economist who appreciates the foundations and limitations of this fundamental framework.

The most important foundation of supply and demand is the concept of balance, or in the economist's jargon *market equilibrium*. Market equilibrium occurs when demand equals supply with the balancing achieved by variations in a product's price.

A market is interpreted no more precisely than as the arena in which those wishing to sell and those wishing to buy a product put their wishes into effect. The market can take place in a specific location and in a formally organized way, as in a stock exchange, or via an unstructured linkage of, for example, people buying and selling new or used cars. However, most markets have formal connections. The formal stock exchange is the focal point of informally linked brokers and stockowners who make a market via a complex network of communications that center on the exchange. Even the informal gold market, with buyers and sellers in almost every country, involves a formal twice-daily price setting in a gold trading room in London.

In order to see how market equilibrium occurs we can ask what happens when it does not occur. In a situation where supply exceeds demand, the economist argues that those suppliers unable to find customers will lower their asking prices to encourage someone to buy what they are offering. People will always buy a product at the lowest price they can find, so if all the buyers know all the sellers' prices, and one seller lowers the price, the remaining sellers will have to reduce their prices. The incentive to lower prices will continue until the increase in quantity demanded caused by the lower prices makes demand equal to the supply. Only then will all the suppliers be able to find buyers. Similarly, if the price is below the level where supply equals demand people will want to buy more than there is available. Economists assume they will bid against each other until the price is again at the level where the quantity demanded equals the quantity supplied.

In the case of a price too high for supply to equal demand economists tend to think that it is competition between sellers that returns the price to where supply and demand are equal. In the case of a price that is too low, it is believed to be competition between the buyers that restores market equilibrium.

Because economists believe prices affect the quantity demanded and the quantity supplied, there are two forces working to establish market equilibrium. When price increases because of an *excess demand,* this lowers the quantity demanded and increases the quantity supplied. Both of these reduce the excess demand. Similarly, if we were to think of starting where the supply exceeds the demand, that is, with *excess supply,* we have two reasons why the decline in price will tend to restore market equilibrium: at a lower price people will demand a larger quantity and producers will offer a smaller quantity for sale.

Generally, the economist likes to check whether an equilibrium is a *stable equilibrium* in the sense that if something disturbs it the equilibrium will eventually be restored. The meaning of stability of equilibrium can be explained by thinking of a ball bearing sitting at the lowest point on a concave surface, a shallow bowl, for example. The ball bearing will be in a stable equilibrium because if we push it away from the lowest point, gravity will help return it there, perhaps after a period of rolling up and down the sides in ever decreasing amounts. If we carefully balance a ball bearing on a convex surface, as on the top of an inverted shallow bowl, and manage to prevent it from rolling off, it would also be in equilibrium. However, this is an *unstable equilibrium* because while it will remain in balance if undisturbed, if it is pushed even a tiny distance from the pinnacle it will roll away and not return to its original position. This should illustrate why supply and demand generally provide a stable equilibrium: if for some reason the price of a product were to be pushed too high causing an excess supply, seller competition would return it to its original level, and if it were to be pushed too low causing an excess demand, competition among buyers would force it up.

A product's price would be difficult to determine not only with an unstable equilibrium, but with what we can define as a *metastable equilibrium*. In terms of our analogy, a ball bearing on a flat, level surface is in a metastable equilibrium and will sit wherever it is put. In the case of supply and demand, a metastable equilibrium would occur if supply and demand were equal at every price. In such a situation, we would never know what would happen to the price if the original metastable equilibrium were disturbed; that is, we would not know where it would settle. Any price could cause quantity supplied to equal the quantity demanded.

It is only if the quantity supplied and demanded has nothing to do with price that metastable equilibrium could occur. However, economists feel confident that the quantity demanded does indeed fall at higher prices because people's buying power is limited; therefore a higher price for a product means giving up the opportunity to buy greater quantities of other products. Similarly, economists feel confident that, in general, firms will produce and/or ship larger quantities at higher prices because firms are interested in maximizing profits. Market stability is hence the result of the assumptions about buyers maximizing their satisfaction with limited incomes, and the suppliers maximizing their profits; that is, the very assumptions we used in the foregoing chapters.

THINKING SMALL

Having established whether an equilibrium is stable, the next step in the economist's way of thinking with supply and demand is to see what the theory implies when exogenous factors change. For instance, the economist might check the implications of an assumed increased demand because of increased incomes. Alternatively, he or she might ask what would happen if the supply of a product were increased because of good weather for an agricultural crop, or because of new developments in manufacturing a product. When a new equilibrium is reached, where supply again equals demand, the economist compares the new market price and quantity with the old to see how the hypothesized change that destroyed the original market equilibrium affects the product's price and quantity traded. This procedure, of destroying equilibrium in a controlled way to see what hypothesized changes will do, we have referred to as comparative statics because it involves comparing two stable, or static, equilibria.

The comparison of equilibria within a particular market, whether it be for wine, gold, oil, used cars, or rare stamps, involves the analysis of a rather limited, narrow economic environment. In reality, events in any market are affected by events in many other markets in a complex, interdependent fashion. Ultimately, all markets are interdependent because of the limits on what people have available to spend. When oil prices increase by a substantial amount, it will affect not only the markets for oil and other sources of energy, as well as the markets for products that use oil like automobiles and industrial machines, but also the markets for food, furniture, and everything else. After all, if you have to pay more for gas there will not be as much left over for buying other goods and services.

Because concentration on supply and demand within an individual market or small number of markets is narrow, the comparison of equilibria, even when some limited interconnections are allowed, is known as *partial-equilibrium analysis*. This contrasts with the much more complex procedure in which all markets are considered simultaneously, which is known as *general-equilibrium analysis*. Ordinary day-to-day economic thinking is generally done within a partial-equilibrium framework because the alternative is complicated, and apart from some basic rules—such as if I spend more than I earn somebody else must do the reverse—involves considerable mathematics. However, it is safe to say that the majority of problems faced in the area of microeconomics, which is what we are dealing with in studying supply and demand, can be handled well with partial-equilibrium analysis. In order to show how incredibly useful it can be in thinking economically, let us have a good time shaking up some equilibria.

Suppose that you have been moved from the production planning to the marketing of the car called The Sting, and that supply and demand have been equal at 5,000 Stings produced and sold per month at a price of $10,000 each. Let us disturb this equilibrium with the introduction of a new, jazzy sportscar from Japan that causes the quantity of Stings sold per month to drop to 4,000.

At the original price of $10,000 and the profit-maximizing output of 5,000 units per month there will be an excess supply. To stimulate demand you might decide to lower the price. This could be done via a buyer's rebate, the inclusion of "free" extras, or a straight sticker price reduction to, perhaps, $9,500. At the lower price, and hence a lower marginal revenue, it will pay to cut back production, perhaps to 4,500 per month. There will also be an increase in the quantity of Stings demanded. If the quantity demanded is also 4,500 per month at the lower price, the market is again in balance or equilibrium. The equilibrium involves a lower quantity and also a lower price.

Let us go back to the original equilibrium with the output of 5,000 cars per month and a price of $10,000 and shake it up again. Suppose this time that as a result of an increase in incomes people want to buy 6,000 Stings at $10,000 each.

A demand for 6,000 Stings when 5,000 are being produced means excess demand. Therefore, you will find that you can increase the price and still sell the 5,000 you are making. Indeed, at the higher price your production manager, if trained in economics, will want to make more. There will be some higher price at which the quantity demanded will equal the quantity supplied. This might be a price of $10,500, at which the supply and demand are both 5,500 units. We find that the increased demand from the higher incomes of buyers has resulted in a higher equilibrium price and a larger quantity produced and sold.

Both disturbances we have considered result from changes in demand. Now let us alter our original equilibrium by changing the supply.

Suppose that auto workers succeed in getting an increase in their wages. This means a higher marginal cost of The Sting, reducing the profit-maximizing output. As you reduce output, there will be excess demand at the original $10,000 price. This will allow you to raise the price a little. You might well end up charging $10,500 and producing 4,500 per month, with the same amount being demanded at the slightly higher price. The new equilibrium from the pro-duction cost increase is a higher price and a reduced quantity supplied and demanded. We would get the reverse effect if marginal costs declined, as they might from productivity gains in the plant. The lower marginal cost increases the profit-maximizing output from the original 5,000 cars to perhaps 5,500, which might lower the price to $9,500. At the lower price the additional 500 cars are purchased. We find a productivity gain has lowered the price and caused more to be produced and bought.

The conclusions we have reached by thinking economically are hardly surprising and are the same conclusions most non-economists would reach. This is probably because the principles of supply and demand have percolated down to the non-economist, as we claimed at the beginning of this chapter. However, while the *qualitative* conclusions are appreciated by non-economists, the economist can reach *quantitative* conclusions that are far from obvious. Indeed, when it comes to the size of the effects of certain types of changes on prices and quantities, we can see how much more we can appreciate when we think economically. In that vein, let us return to the effect of productivity improvements on equilibrium prices and quantities.

In our example, we assumed that the improvement in productivity resulted in a price of $9,500 and sales of 5,500 units. In the original equilibrium the price had been $10,000 and sales 5,000. The total revenue from selling the car has therefore increased to $52,250,000, or $9,500 × 5,500, from the original level of $50,000,000 or $10,000 × 5,000. But could it be that the price of the car could fall so much relative to the extra quantity sold that the total revenue might decline?

It might seem that the new equilibrium of 5,500 units sold at $9,500 is no more likely than a new equilibrium with the same price of $9,500, but with a quantity of 5,200 cars per month. After all, the lower price has increased demand in this case, even if only slightly. Yet if this other equilibrium did occur, total revenue would be reduced by the gain in productivity, falling from $50,000,000 to $49,400,000. However, economic thinking tells us that in the case of a product like The Sting, for which the producer determines the profit-maximizing output, total revenue could not decline from a lower price and higher quantity.

The economist reasons as follows: The profit-maximizing level of output is where marginal cost and marginal revenue are equal. Marginal cost is obviously always positive; it cannot cost a negative amount to produce an extra car or else it would pay to produce cars even if their price were zero. But if marginal cost is positive, marginal revenue must be positive when they are being equalized. By definition, positive marginal revenue—the increase in revenue from an extra sale—means that total revenue increases when more are sold, despite the fact that in order to sell more the price must be reduced.

Total revenue increases when sales increase only if the percentage increase in sales exceeds the percentage decrease in price that causes this. In our primary example, sales increase by 10 percent while price decreases by 5 percent. The economist refers to this as *elastic demand,* because the quantity sold is sensitive to the price. (When demand does not change as much as the price and is therefore inflexible, the economist says demand is *inelastic.*) What we have found is that no firm that can influence its output, and thereby market prices, will produce an output where demand is inelastic. Because they have positive marginal revenue they must face elastic demand.

We can view the foregoing conclusion another way. As we have explained, inelastic demand means the percentage increase in quantity demanded is smaller than the reduction in price that brings this about. Therefore, it also means that when prices increase the quantity demanded decreases by a smaller amount than the price increases. It is clear that if prices increase more than quantity decreases, total revenue is increased. This means that a firm facing an inelastic demand could increase its revenues by cutting back its production. Cutting back production also lowers costs. With higher revenues and lower costs profits are larger, so we know a firm could not be maximizing profits if it is producing an output level where the demand is inelastic.

Few, if any, non-economists would be likely to reach the foregoing conclusion that an individual firm would never face an inelastic demand because it requires very careful reasoning about quantitative effects. However, it is not only on the quantitative effects that thinking economically helps. Even on the qualitative side, that is, on the direction of changes in prices and output from changes in supplies and demands, non-economists frequently reach different conclusions than economists. This is because thinking economically helps us avoid a common error made by non-economists. But what is this error?

Returning to our example of The Sting, we will recall that an increase in demand brought about by higher incomes of buyers increased the price from $10,000 to $10,500 per car, but despite the higher price, people ended up buying more of them—sales grew from 5,000 to 5,500 per month. However, when we were discussing demand earlier, we said that at higher prices the quantity demanded declines. Is there an inconsistency in arguing for higher demand at

$10,500 per car than at $10,000, while at the same time arguing that higher prices lower quantity demanded?

There is no inconsistency in what we have said because we are dealing with different things. When the demand for The Sting increases from increased buyer incomes we are talking of an increase in demand at all prices. When people have more disposable income they want to buy more cars if they are $10,000 each, and more if they are $10,500 each. However, even after their interest in The Sting has been enhanced by an increased income, they will continue to demand a lower quantity at $10,500 each than at $10,000 each. The latter is the traditional effect of prices on the quantity demanded that we met earlier.

The important distinction we are using is the distinction we explained in chapter 3, namely between a "change in demand," brought about by something other than the product's price, and a "change in the quantity demanded," brought about by changing the product's price. Whenever demand is changed by something other than the product's price—such as buyers' incomes—the new equilibrium price and quantity supplied will both be higher (as from a demand increase) or both be lower (as from a demand decrease) than they were. However, when we change the product's price in order to see what happens, the quantity demanded changes in opposite direction to the price. To help minimize the difficulties in determining what sort of change we are considering, we have already explained that we use "increases in demand" and "decreases in demand" whenever talking of changes in factors other than the product's price. When changing the product's price we talk of the consequent "increase in quantity demanded" or "decrease in quantity demanded."

There are a number of factors that we introduced in chapter 3 that can change demand. For example, a decrease in the price of a substitute product—a product that fulfills a similar function—will cause a decline in demand. A substitute for The Sting might be a Japanese car, and if a Japanese car became cheaper fewer Stings would be bought at every price. Demand is also decreased by an increased price of complements—products enjoyed jointly. For example, more expensive gasoline would reduce the demand for Stings, unless it is regarded as a particularly fuel-efficient car. The effects of substitute and complement prices are in addition to the effects of income and "tastes," with the latter the catchall that helps economists cover all eventualities.

Supply is changed from such factors as input prices and productivity, which affect marginal cost. We have seen how these changes work. Supply is also affected by taxes on output paid by producers, which effectively also mean changes in marginal cost. With agricultural products supply is changed by the weather, the chance invasion by pests, and so on. All these changes influence the quantity supplied, whatever the price.

When the price of a product is increased we say this *increases the quantity supplied.* On the other hand, when more is supplied because of something other than the product's own price, perhaps because of a reduction in marginal cost, we say there is an *increase in supply.*

To make sure you understand the distinction between changes in supply and demand, and changes in the quantity supplied and demanded, let us examine a common incorrect answer to the economics question, "Explain what happens after an increase in demand." Economics professors, having been convinced they have conveyed the workings of supply and demand correctly, are often driven wild when they hear an answer that goes:

"After an increase in demand there is an excess demand. Consequently, competition among buyers leads them to offer a higher price to satisfy their demands. This causes producers to make and send more to market. The increased supply in turn puts downward pressure on the price. This causes increased demand, which causes the price to go up. The higher price induces producers to add to their output, which causes excess supply and a consequent drop in price, which raises demand. . . ."

And so on, *ad nauseum*. Obviously, something has gone wrong and we have gotten into an infinite loop. Can you spot the points where the important distinctions are not being made?

The point where the erroneous answer begins to go astray is where it was said that "the increased supply in turn puts downward pressure on prices." The reference to more being sent to market is not an increase in supply, but an increase in the quantity supplied. The increase in quantity supplied is the result of an increase in the product's price. It cannot, therefore, lower the product's price if it is the result of an increase in the product's price. This is a clear contradiction. If the answer had ended when it was said that "this causes producers to make and send more to market," it would have been correct. The original increase in demand would then leave a higher price and a larger quantity demanded and supplied. By continuing to reason beyond this point we have strayed into uneconomic thinking.

There is a rather limited sense in which the erroneous answer could be considered to have some validity. However, for this to be the case we must explicitly introduce lags in the response of supply to price changes, as in the cases of the markets for oil and for astrophysicists.

With strong oil demand in the late 1960s and 1970s, and supply restrictions by the members of the Organization of Petroleum Exporting Countries (OPEC), the price of oil rose very rapidly. It took some time, but the high price gave the non-OPEC countries an incentive to look for and develop oil reserves and eventually, by the 1980s, their excess supply depressed prices. This removed the strong incentive to develop reserves, an effect which should eventually reduce oil supply forcing prices up again.

In the case of astrophysicists, high demand and good salaries in the 1960s sent many students with the best minds into lengthy graduate programs. Years later, so many graduated at once that there were insufficient jobs, serving to dampen salaries and discourage others from becoming astrophysicists.

If you are now wondering why, with such good salaries for accountants, for instance, there has not been a rush into accounting programs causing a subsequent salary decline and cobweb cycle like that experienced by astrophysicists, the economist may have an answer. (Adaption of old theories to fit new evidence is the way of all sciences.) The economist might argue that while accountants do have a high pecuniary income the nonpecuniary returns from their jobs are rather poor. Perhaps an accounting career would be considered boring to a large number of people, lacking the glamour of a career as an astrophysicist. The high income is therefore not a temporary aberration, but part of a long-run equilibrium. (We are probably beginning to realize that economists will resort to almost anything to explain what doesn't fit their theories and what they cannot explain they will attribute to such factors as tastes or psychic income, explanations which are very difficult to reject via empirical observation.)

CHAPTER 8

Thinking Tentatively

Limitations of
Supply and Demand

Management is known by the company it keeps.
Anonymous

The worst crime against working people is a company
which fails to operate at a profit.
SAMUEL GOMPERS

IN CHAPTER 2 we listed the final step in the economist's
approach to a problem as the testing of the implications
derived from the assumptions. It would seem that with all
the data we have on prices and quantities, testing of the
law of supply and demand would not be difficult. Unfortunately, however, the data that we can observe cannot be
used directly to test the validity of the law of supply and
demand. Higher prices are not always observed along with
lower quantities, which would appear to support our
thinking on demand. Nor do higher prices always occur
with larger quantities, which would appear to support our
thinking on supply. What we observe are equilibria, not
the simultaneously occurring behavior behind the equilibria,
and it is difficult to induce what the two sides of supply

and demand that cause market outcomes are from the outcomes themselves. It is rather like trying to determine from the observation of a large number of goals scored by a team, whether this is the result of a good attack by the team, or of a poor defense by their opponents.

The difficulty of testing supply and demand from their outcomes is known to econometricians, not surprisingly, as the *identification problem.* While it is a problem generally faced only by the econometrician, it is important that everyone who thinks economically appreciates this difficulty. Otherwise, you might be led from, say, the observation of low oil prices and low oil consumption to reject the theory of demand, when the outcome is the result of low demand. Alternatively, you might conclude from higher oil prices and low production that the supply theory is incorrect, when in fact the outcome is due to a low supply. There is no reason whatsoever for market prices and quantities to be observed moving in any particular direction relative to each other. When people quote the path of prices and quantities in an attempt to disprove the economic thinking about supply or demand, they are revealing they do not know how economists think.

Apart from errors the non-economist may make in trying to verify supply and demand from market observations, or from confusing changes in supply and demand with changes in quantities supplied and demanded, the fundamental laws are in most cases correctly applied. "It's the result of the laws of supply and demand" is the everyday answer to inquiries about price changes, whether we are questioning the grocer about the cost of lettuce or a specialist about the price of gold. We might well wonder, however, whether it is inconsistent for the same people who cite supply and demand to explain price setting in other ways. For example, it is not at all uncommon to hear firms claim that they charge whatever their competitors are charging so as to prevent their customers from shopping elsewhere. It is also common for firms to excuse price increases for their products by saying that their costs have increased. Explicit in the latter statement is that they are pricing as a markup over costs, not directly according to supply and demand. Since these views may be held by the same people who cite supply and demand, and are held by many non-economists, we may well ask if this reveals any fundamental inconsistencies. Are markup pricing and charging the same as the competition examples of uneconomic thinking?

Some of the apparent inconsistency in views on pricing can be explained by the difference between the establishment of market prices for an industry and the pricing of the individual firms that constitute an industry. While the market price of wheat is indeed determined by the forces of supply and demand, the price that any individual wheat farmer can charge is outside the farmer's control. If a farmer charged even a tiny amount over the going market price for a particular quality of produce, none would be sold. Alternatively, if an individual farmer withheld some of his or her output to force up the market price, he or she would be poorer than by selling everything at the going price. Therefore, it follows that farmers are best off taking the market price as given and selling everything at that price.

While each individual farmer may think prices are set by the competition, they are really being set by market supply and demand. It would be fallacious to think that because each farmer takes the market price as given that there is nothing to set this price. The explanation of pricing is, and most definitely should be, different from the perspective of the firm than it is from the perspective of the industry, and it takes a certain appreciation of economic thinking to step between these two levels. There is no inconsistency if we preserve supply and demand for industry pricing, but allow each firm to set prices according to what the competition is setting.

The markup view of pricing can be stated in terms very similar to that of "pricing according to the competition." To do this we can think of the owners of firms requiring a return from their investment that is appropriate for the effort and risk they take. If all different firms face similar costs and similar risks they will preserve their returns if each individual firm sets prices at, say, 10 percent over their costs. They will then all be charging the same price while this is set according to industry supply and demand. Each firm would be merely using as a rule of thumb the standard rate of markup for that industry, and they would all be charging what the competition is charging.

The fact that market prices are set by industry supply and demand, while each individual firm in a competitive industry takes prices as given, helps explain a phenomenon that has baffled many a non-economist, that of improved agricultural revenues in some years of bad harvests.

Bad harvests improve each firm's revenues, and therefore total industry revenues, if the reduction in industry supply is smaller than the price increase it causes. This, by definition, means that the demand faced by the entire industry is inelastic. (Recall that inelastic demand occurs when quantity demanded declines by a smaller percentage than prices increase.) This inelastic demand of the industry can co-exist with an elastic demand facing each firm in the industry. Indeed, because each firm in a competitive industry must sell at the going price or sell nothing, the demand facing each individual firm is infinitely elastic. This is because the demand declines by an infinite amount from the smallest increase in the firm's price if it is not matched by other firms.

While there are ways of reconciling different views of pricing for the industry and the firm in an industry, there are some elements of price setting that call the fundamental theory into question. Two limitations to the general applicability of the law of supply and demand come from the practices of selling at advertised prices that are infrequently revised, and from the introduction of non-market considerations into the marketplace.

Because supply and demand are likely to be continually changing, even if by only minor amounts, we would also expect to see market prices continually changing. This certainly appears to be the case for such freely traded commodities as fresh produce, meat, fish, stocks and bonds, gold, and a vast volume of wholesale items. However, there are a number of goods and services that are sold according to listed prices that are only infrequently revised. For example, list prices of automobiles, books, movie tickets, and ballpoint pens often remain unchanged for months on end. This might appear to indicate that the law of supply and demand is not determining prices at every point in time, but does it mean the law is incorrect?

Prices may be fixed for lengthy periods to prevent buyers from being upset by uncertainty about them. Imagine never knowing the cost of school tuition, or of a movie, until the actual moment of payment. Until it is clear that a sustained price increase is warranted by long-run supply and demand conditions, many firms are reluctant to announce new prices, which not only creates uncertainty for customers, but which may, in effect, be expensive to convey to actual or potential buyers. It follows that the presence of published prices does not mean that prices are determined without consideration of supply and demand. Rather it may mean it is expensive to change prices either in terms of customer goodwill or in terms of the cost of advertising new prices.

Sometimes the reluctance to change prices in response to changing market conditions is the result of fear about how other firms in the industry may react. In *oligopolistic* industries, which are those involving a limited number of firms producing and selling products like detergents or gasoline which are products where each firm's output differs little from that of other firms other than by brand, firms must calculate whether their own price change will be matched or even exceeded. If the firm is the only seller raising its price it may find all its customers going elsewhere. If it lowers its price it may touch off a price war. Because it can be costly to increase prices if the change is not matched by other firms in the industry—all the customers going elsewhere—and costly to lower them if this sparks a price war, we may find prices moving only hesitantly toward the levels dictated by supply and demand. However, as in the case of prices that are costly to advertise, in the long run prices will be changed. We discover that supply and demand remains an important tool for thinking economically, even when we have price lists that are difficult to change or an oligopolistic market. The only limitation is that we do have a more difficult job explaining the timing of price changes.

Many prices are clearly not explained by the unfettered working of supply and demand because they are set or limited by the government, an agency, a trade union, a cartel, or some other regulatory body. For example, rents may be limited by a rent control authority, wages by minimum wage laws or by union contracts, agricultural prices by support programs, interest rates by ceilings on lending or deposit rates, and so on. However, while interferences in the marketplace do limit the applicability of supply and demand in explaining prices, economic thinking is in many ways still helped by having the law of supply and demand to use in appreciating the consequences of these market impediments. It will do us no harm to see what the law of supply and demand tells us about pricing restrictions and of the danger of playing with the powerful forces of supply and demand.

To begin, let us think of how an economist would analyze the effects of minimum wage laws. Because these laws are effective only if they keep wages above the level they would otherwise have been, the economist thinks of their effects in terms of having a price—the price of labor or wage—above the level for market equilibrium. Put differently, the economist thinks of the effects of minimum wages in terms of the effect of having wages above the level where the supply and demand for labor are equal. (This wage is frequently referred to as the *full-employment wage.*) If the wage is too high, the demand for workers by employees will be lower than without the minimum wage law, while the number wanting to work at these wages is greater than it would otherwise have been. The result will be an excess supply in the labor market.

An excess supply in the labor market means some people

without work, so the economist thinks of the consequence of minimum wage laws as being higher wages for those who find work, but zero wages for others, who generally are the unskilled. From a positive economic standpoint we cannot say the laws ought to be abolished (a normative statement based on normative thinking) because there are some who benefit. We can, however, unequivocally state that the effort to be fair to poorly paid workers can be extremely unfair to those who would like to work, but who are prevented from doing so. For example, college students interested in part-time jobs in restaurants or pumping gas, and older people willing to work as caretakers or janitors could be forced out of making a little extra to help them along. At the higher minimum wage there is often an incentive to introduce machines to do away with the need to hire labor. For example, as a response to high wage rates we may find a move toward self-service gas stations, mechanical dish-washers, electrical security surveillance systems, and cleaning machines such as built-in industrial vacuums and mechanical sweepers.

To many, the use of machines in the place of demeaning work is a fine substitute for labor. However, the unemployed may think differently. From the point of view of positive economic thinking, we can explain only the consequences of minimum wage laws. This may help us decide if we think we ought to abolish the laws. Positive economics is therefore useful in the normative arena which makes the distinction between positive and normative thinking extremely fuzzy when the distinction is pushed to the limit.

We can apply the same type of analysis to explain the effects of agricultural price support programs as we just used to explain the consequences of minimum wage laws. To the extent that agricultural prices are kept higher than they would have been, we again have a situation of excess supply; the higher prices increase supply, and if they are passed on to the consumer they reduce the quantity demanded. There may be a benefit to farmers from a higher return, but this must be balanced against the potentially higher cost to the consumer. Moreover, in order to keep the price artificially high the government must continue to buy the excess production. Storage may eventually become an expensive, troublesome problem.

To the other extreme of keeping prices high, as with minimum wage laws and agricultural price supports, we have situations where prices are kept artificially low. For example, rent controls are an attempt to prevent tenants from being abused by landlords while usury laws are an attempt to prevent lenders from taking advantage of borrowers.

Rent controls, to the extent that they succeed in keeping rents down, mean the price of accommodation is below equilibrium. Supply will therefore be lower than it would have been while demand is higher. Supply is lower, especially in the longer run, because landlords will have a reduced incentive to provide new accommodation; they may even allow existing rental accommodation to deteriorate if new housing is exempt of controls. Demand is higher because people prefer the controlled units to the uncontrolled units. There may well be a gain for those lucky in finding controlled housing, but this must be weighed against the lower supply and illicit schemes likely to crop up, such as "key money" and "favors" demanded of tenants by landlords.

Usury laws work somewhat like rent controls. By having interest rates lower than the equilibrium level where the supply of funds equals the demand, the quantity supplied is reduced while the quantity demanded is increased. Some borrowers will be unable to find loans, while those who find them will benefit. The limited supply of funds is likely to be rationed, with those offering the best security and who are generally wealthier, getting the most loans.

Again, there are gainers and losers from usury laws. So while positive economic thinking can identify their consequences, it cannot of itself decide on whether the laws should be scrapped. This is a political decision, as before. However, the conclusions of applying positive economic thinking could be and are usefully employed in arguing against the usury laws, again linking positive and normative economics.

Fairness and other non-market considerations which influence regulators of wages and prices limit the power of positive economic thinking because we have no theory of what the regulators consider fair. However, without such a theory, there will be a lot in our economic environment we cannot explain, greatly reducing the value of economics.

Fairness is a relative rather than an absolute concept and involves making normative decisions. For example, in the market for labor the fairness of a wage, which may be set by a labor arbitrator, is judged by comparing it to the wages of others and imposing a belief about how they ought to differ. What constitutes a fair wage for a fireman is likely to be defined by reference to the wage of a policeman, and so on. (This can result in a wage-led inflationary situation if each side levers against the other, and causes difficulties when both sides simultaneously succeed in achieving wage settlements offering more than the other. This actually happened for the firemen and policemen of a major U.S. city.)

Many prices in addition to wages are determined in a

nonmarket manner. Property taxes, postal rates, telephone charges, electricity prices, and so on, are set at least in part in an arena outside that of supply and demand. However, economic thinking can still be applied even if it leads us into the normative questions of how regulators have traditionally determined, for example, fair rates of return for shareholders of utilities and the prices of electricity, telephone, and so forth these warrant. Most often, fair rates of return are based on the risk the shareholders are forced to accept because the risk cannot be reduced by diversifying investments. There is sufficient consistency in the way regulatory bodies have acted in determining fair utility prices, and in the way arbitrators have determined fair wages, that these could be incorporated into economics even if we have to make assumptions about how fairness is judged (taking us into normative thinking).

When markets are free and not governed by government controls or notions of fairness there is still the problem of whether prices really will find their equilibrium where supply equals demand. Even if there is a new equilibrium and even if it is stable when it is reached, what guarantees we will reach it? In other words, while we can compare equilibria— the basis of comparative statics—can we be sure we move from equilibrium to equilibrium? This is a question of dynamics, a subject economists rarely study. It is clear that if we never reach equilibria, the power of economic thinking is greatly diminished.

A closely related problem to that of concentrating on comparative statics is the problem of there being such frequent disturbances to equilibria, even if the dynamics are leading there, that we never actually reach them. We are always at prices and quantities that are tending toward equilibrium rather than at the equilibrium itself. The economist answers that while this may be true it still helps to think economically if it tells us where we are heading.

Nonmarket pricing and difficulties in reaching equilibria aside, economic thinking is greatly enhanced by the very straightforward framework of supply and demand. Moreover, even in these difficult situations, we can learn something by thinking economically whether it be the effects of price regulations or the nature of the approaching equilibrium. However, what must always be borne in mind is that positive economic thinking tells us nothing about the tastes behind demand or the technology behind supply. This greatly limits our performance in forecasting. Until we integrate some of what is currently taken as being exogenous, economic thinking cannot be a substitute for a crystal ball.

CHAPTER 9

Thinking
Opportunistically

The Determination
of Wages and Rents

> There is no such thing as a free lunch.
> An academic economist

> Time is money.
> A professional economist

IF YOU ASKED someone not trained in economics what determines how much you can earn the person would be likely to list a number of factors: the amount of education you have received, whether you are a member of a trade union or a professional association, how old you are, and how good you are at what you do. However, he or she would be very unlikely to mention the market price of what it is that you produce. This is because non-economists tend to believe it is wages that determine the prices of what labor produces rather than the other way around. We might hear, for example, that automobiles are increasing in price because of a large increase in auto workers' wages, not that wages are moving up because of higher car prices.

127

Similarly, we might be told that other "factor prices," such as rent on land or the cost of raw materials, are forcing up prices of final products, rather than the reverse. For instance, it is not uncommon to hear that fresh produce is costing more because prices of farm land and other farming costs are increasing. This direction of causation of effect from costs to prices seems natural because it starts with the inputs and works toward the outputs. However, it is incorrect.

The economist thinks about wages and other factor prices in terms of the supply and demand of the productive factors. Demand is viewed as *derived* from the demands for final products while supply is determined by the opportunity costs of the factors of production. When there are low opportunity costs, that is, when the factors would not earn much in an alternative use, economists believe that the prices of final products determine factor prices rather than the reverse. They believe, for example, that when land can be used only for a particular crop, and therefore faces no opportunity cost, it will be expensive as a result of the crop fetching a high price. The economist's way of thinking is by no means straightforward and in order to follow it we should begin by carefully explaining the importance of opportunity cost.

You will recall from chapter 3 that in the context of demand opportunity cost is what we are forced to give up by buying what we do. In particular, it is the utility, or satisfaction received, in the next best use of our income. In the case of economic thinking about wages, the opportunity cost that is relevant is the wage we give up by selecting the job we do. The wage we forgo that is relevant is the next highest wage we could have earned had we not chosen our current occupation or our current job.

Economists reason that you are paid by your current employer at least what you are worth to some other employer. If you could earn more elsewhere then, from a purely monetary point of view, you would not stay long in your current job. Since what you could earn elsewhere is the opportunity cost of your current job, the wage you receive depends on your opportunity cost. This view is not inconsistent with what non-economists think because what you would get paid by somebody else will depend on whether you have a degree, how good you are at your job, and so on. However, the economist's way of thinking does help us explain some things that non-economists frequently find perplexing, such as the incomes of baseball players and movie stars.

To an economist, a baseball player's income is high because for a particular team to get a player they must pay at least what he is worth to some other team. If a player has reached "free-agent" status and can therefore move at his own discretion, his value is apparent from the maximum price that other teams are willing to pay. If a baseball player has not been with his draft team sufficient years to have achieved free-agent status his income may not reflect his value to other teams, but his transfer price will. This is because good draft players who are put on the market will solicit bidding from a number of teams, and the successful bidder must pay a little more than the maximum that others would bid. The difference is that free agents collect their own benefits from competitive bidding, while the draft teams collect on those who are not free agents.

There are few non-economists who would have been

able to explain the baseball player's income, at least if they depended on the sort of factors we listed at the opening of this chapter. After all, the income has little to do with the number of years of education or the presence of a baseball player's union. However, the economic way of thinking not only explains the wages of baseball players but can also explain wages of ordinary people where education and other factors do make a difference. For example, the economist would reason that when a person acquires valuable skills from earning an M.B.A. numerous firms will value these skills, and it becomes necessary to pay at least what other firms are prepared to pay, namely, the M.B.A.'s opportunity cost. Therefore, the economist's way of thinking is consistent with the view of most non-economists.

But isn't there a problem with the economist's viewpoint? Doesn't the answer that we "are paid at least what we are worth to somebody else" merely put the problem back a step? What determines what we are worth to others? As you might suspect, the economist is not without an answer.

Economists argue that what a person is worth to some other firm is the amount he or she contributes to that firm's profits. Because profits are defined as the difference between total revenue and total cost, economists reason that people are hired if they add to revenue more than they are paid.

The amount that an employee adds to a company's revenues is referred to as the worker's *marginal revenue product,* or MRP. The term "marginal" is used because we are measuring the contribution of an extra worker, and "product" is used because his or her contribution is made by increasing production. The middle word "revenue" is used because the contribution to revenue of the worker's extra production is what we are measuring. Because a firm hires people if they add to company profits, we can say they are hired as long as their MRP exceeds their wage rate. If an additional auto worker can help produce an extra four cars per year that bring in a total additional revenue to the car company of $20,000 net of other variable costs like steel and so on, the worker is worth hiring provided his or her wage rate is below $20,000. Similarly if a baseball player brings in extra gate receipts of $1 million per season, the player is worth paying up to $1 million a season.

Because economists assume companies maximize their profits, they reason that no firm would fail to hire extra workers if the workers' MRPs exceeded their wages. If they did not hire workers whose MRPs exceeded their wages they would not be maximizing because extra workers would make profits even higher. Therefore, economic thinking leads us to conclude that firms will continue hiring until the last, or marginal, person hired has an MRP equal to his or her wage. But how does the economist know such a level of employment is eventually reached?

If we go back to the law of diminishing returns, we find that after some point additional workers are not as productive as workers previously hired; there is only so much more we can squeeze from a given-sized factory. In addition, as more is produced, the price of the final product declines. With lower output from extra workers and lower prices of output the MRP must eventually decline. At some level of employment we reach a point where the marginal or last person has an MRP equal to the wage rate.

If a worker's output were clearly attributable to his or

her own effort and product prices were uninfluenced by company output, as in competitive markets, we could think of the worker's MRP as being made up of the amount he or she produces and the price, net of other variable costs, at which it is sold. If we really could say the marginal auto worker adds four cars per year to company output, then this is the worker's *marginal physical product,* or MPP. To convert this into the MRP, we multiply MPP by the price, net of all other variable costs of the cars they produce. If cars are sold from the factory at a constant $10,000 each, netting $5,000 after costs of steel, plastic, and so on, we get an MRP of an additional worker of 4 × $5,000, or $20,000. This then helps us explain what changes the amount workers can earn.

Within any given labor market, the higher the price of the final product that a worker produces the higher will be the wage that firms are prepared to pay. If a car produced by some competing car manufacturer went up in price by $2,000, but material costs remained unchanged, the MRP of an additional worker to the competing firm, if it also gets four extra cars per extra employee, would increase by $8,000. The competitor would therefore offer a higher wage and each other car firm would have to pay more or lose employees. This says that the value of labor is determined, at least in part, by the value of what workers produce, albeit in some other firm, a conclusion quite different from that reached by many non-economists.

In addition to the value, or price, of a worker's output, the MRP is made up of the worker's productivity as reflected in the marginal physical product. As the MPP to an employer increases this will increase what they will pay. Therefore, other employers will also have to pay more. If in a particular automobile company a worker's productivity increases to 5 cars per year, perhaps because better machinery is employed, then, at the original $5,000 net each, the worker will be worth $25,000 per year. Every employer will have to offer this to prevent the worker from going to the employer where the worker's productivity has increased.

The conclusion that a worker's wage goes up if his or her productivity increases should not be news to many non-economists. However, they may be surprised by the conclusion that wages will go up even if the productivity increase is because their employer or some other employer bought better machinery. Why doesn't investment in new machinery benefit employers rather than workers, and only these employers who invested in the machinery? Economic thinking about wages makes this clear: A worker's wages are increased in all firms or else those that do invest in the productivity increasing machinery will bid the workers away from those that don't. But does this mean that it doesn't pay to invest in better machinery?

It is true that some of the productivity gains from better machines are enjoyed by workers rather than by firms, even when the workers' own firms did not invest. However, if any firm failed to keep its production technology up to date it would quickly become uncompetitive. It follows that even if all the productivity gains were competed away via higher wages, each firm would still be forced to invest. Moreover, as we have seen, in equilibrium they will get a return in the form of the *normal rate of return* on investments. Otherwise, firms would exit from the business, lowering total market supply and raising prices until those firms that remain do get such a return. Also, investors can enjoy above normal returns before the new equilibrium is restored.

THINKING SMALL

Thinking economically on productivity provides another insight, about on-the-job training. The economist's way of thinking is based on the fact that what a firm must pay is a worker's MRP to some other potential employer. It therefore distinguishes between on-the-job training that makes a worker of more value to only the firm that trains its employees, called *firm-specific on-the-job training,* and training that makes the worker of more value to other firms, called *general on-the-job training.*

General on-the-job training, which raises the worker's MRP elsewhere, will not help the firm providing the training. It will induce other firms to compete to take the worker away from the firm that paid for the education. To prevent the employee from leaving, the firm that paid for the training would therefore also be forced to raise wages by the improved MRP. It follows that providing workers with training of general benefit will not increase profits. Profits would be increased only if the worker's additional contribution to revenue exceeded the addition to cost, but competition from outside will prevent this from happening.

Job-specific training which increases the worker's MRP only to the firm providing training, like knowledge about the way that firm operates, can be worthwhile. This is because it has no effect on MRPs elsewhere and therefore the benefit is not used up in higher wages forced on the firm by competition from outside.

Thinking about wages as being at least what some other employer would pay, which is the worker's MRP to that employer, helps us explain both the supply of workers to an individual firm and the supply to a labor market; when the worker's opportunity costs in a particular labor market increase the labor supply in that market declines. However, knowing labor supply doesn't tell us the market wage. In order to get the market wage in addition to labor supply we need labor demand. We can then find the price, or wage, where the supply and demand for labor are equal. Whereas labor supply depends on MRPs and hence opportunity costs in other markets, labor demand depends on MRPs in the market itself.

The total market demand for a particular category of workers, whether it be newly graduated M.B.A.'s or experienced baseball players, is the sum of the individual demands of all the separate employers of that category of worker. The total, or market, demand for professional baseball players is the sum of the demands of all professional baseball teams. At each wage there will be a different number demanded by each team, and therefore by all teams collectively. The higher the market wage the fewer players each team will want to hire and, therefore, the lower the effective quantity of baseball players demanded.

Because different workers face different opportunity costs the quantity of labor supplied to a particular labor market will also depend on wages. As in the general case of supply, the higher the wage in a particular labor market the higher the number of people who are likely to find this exceeding their opportunity cost and, therefore, the higher the quantity of labor supplied. (However, there is a chance that wages could get so high that people would demand more leisure and therefore the hours people would want to work could actually fall. Generally, however, we assume this will not happen.)

The market wage resulting from the interaction of supply and demand in a particular labor market will mean that some workers are just, and only just, willing to supply their labor at that wage. However, others would have been willing to have supplied their labor even if the wage had been lower.

The difference between what a person earns, that is, the market wage, and what would have induced him or her to supply their labor to a particular market is referred to as that worker's *economic rent*. Economic rent is the payment to a factor of production—such as labor or land—over and above that necessary for the factor to be supplied to the market. The size of the economic rent depends on how broadly we interpret the particular market. For example, when we mean the labor market in general a worker's economic rent is the difference between what he or she is earning and what the worker would require to be prepared to work at all. Because the alternative to working means staying at home, receiving little or no income, economic rent will be large and almost equal to the total wage earned. However, if by the market we mean something rather narrow, like the auto workers' market, economic rent is much smaller; it is merely the difference between what the person earns as an auto worker and what he or she could earn in their next best employment opportunity. The more narrowly we define a market, the smaller the economic rent the worker or other factor collects.

Despite the vague nature of the concept of economic rent without making it clear what we mean by "the market," the concept is extremely useful for thinking about the direction of causation between payments to factors of production and the prices of what they produce. We have seen that with cars there is at least some influence running from car prices to auto workers' wages. But is this the only direction of causation or do the wages of auto workers also affect prices of automobiles—or a bit of both? The answer is that the causation is exclusively from final product prices to factor prices only when all the income of a factor is economic rent. We can illustrate this by considering the rent on land, from which the term was borrowed.

According to economic thinking, rent on land is determined just like wages, and indeed, wages can be thought of as the "rental" rate for labor. There is a demand for land that is determined by its MRP. This is in turn determined by its MPP and the price of the final product the land produces. For example, if an acre of land produces 2,000 pounds of potatoes each year—its MPP—netting 25 cents per pound after labor and capital costs, the land would be worth renting as long as the rent was below $500. Land has diminishing MPPs not because of a fixed factor of production but because there is only so much fertile land, and after the best land is in use extra employed acres will not be of as high a quality. Therefore, the higher the rent the fewer the number of acres farmers would find profitable to rent, and the lower the quantity of land demanded.

To find the market rent we also need the supply of land. Traditional economic thinking has the supply as fixed. As Will Rogers said, "Land is a good investment. They ain't making no more." If this is so, and if land would therefore be available for renting whatever was paid, everything the landowner receives is economic rent. If other potato land is paid $500 per acre but would have been rented for potato farming even if the rent was zero, all the $500 received is economic rent. Of course, it is paid $500 despite that fact because it is worth $500 to other farmers who compete for it until the rent is $500.

If land is available for growing potatoes whatever the rent so that all rent is economic rent, the price of potatoes determines the rent on potato land. In our example, with potatoes at 25 cents per pound the rent is $500 per year. If (net) potato prices increased to 50 cents per pound the rent on land would also increase. Indeed, with an MPP of 2,000 pounds the rent would increase to $1,000 per year. We find the rental rate on the factor of production moving proportionately with the price of what the factor produces, with the direction here exclusively from potato prices to the rent on land.

As another example, think of a $1 million per year baseball player who would be a baseball player even if paid only $20,000 per year, and consider the player's economic rent in the baseball player market. Because virtually all this income—$980,000 of it—is economic rent, we can draw the same conclusion as we did for potato growing land. The player earns a lot because people will buy tickets to the game to see him. It is not that ticket prices are determined by what baseball players cost the teams, because they would still be playing even at much lower salaries. However, this isn't so when a factor's payment is not entirely economic rent. We can see this if we consider auto workers earning $20,000 in the industry who could earn about the same assembling computer hardware.

Suppose that because of an expansion in the computer industry causing higher prices—or higher MPPs—of workers, wages paid to computer assemblers increase to $25,000 per year. This would cause workers with small economic rents in the auto industry to jump over. The reduced supply of auto workers would force up their market wage. In addition, the drop in automobile output would force up prices of cars. We find a direction of causation running from factor prices to product prices. Of course, if there were no alternative opportunities for auto workers so that their entire wage was economic rent we wouldn't have wage rates impacting on prices, and auto workers' wages would be determined only by car prices, not vice versa.

In reality, no factor payment is entirely economic rent, even with land. There is always an opportunity cost of the factor in an activity and this must be netted out of what it is paid to find its economic rent. For example, if potato land could also be used for grazing, the supply of potato land would not be fixed. If the land suddenly became more valuable for grazing this would reduce the amount used for growing potatoes and reduce the supply of potatoes. In this case the price of the factor of production increases causing potato prices to rise.

Even when there is no opportunity cost of a factor of production in some other use there's an opportunity cost of letting somebody else use a factor of production versus the owner using the factor him or herself. Indeed, every resource, including labor, has a minimum rent or wage determined by the value of the resource to its owner. For example, even if there were only a solitary buyer of a person's services—a most uncommon situation called *monopsony*— we would not expect the wage to reach zero; most people would prefer sitting in the garden or spending time painting the house to a zero wage. The value of these alternatives determines the wage at which a worker would no longer supply services to the market, and it is referred to as the *reservation wage*. Therefore, even if the labor market we are considering is the market in general not all wages are economic rent; therefore, factor prices can affect product prices. The higher the cost of having somebody else paint the house, and the nicer the weather for sitting in the garden, the higher are workers' reservation wages and the higher the prices are of the final outputs the workers could otherwise have produced.

The implication of owners of factors of production being able to use their factors themselves rather than sell them carries over to ordinary final products and is an important part of thinking economically. If you own a Sting automobile it is the value to you that determines the minimum price at which you would be prepared to sell. It does not matter if you paid $5,000 or $50,000 for it. Only if the market price of used Stings exceeds what it is worth to you would you sell.

When we deal with final products the analogous concept to that of economic rent is called *consumer surplus*. This is the difference between the value of a product to a buyer and what the buyer has to pay for it. Potentially, a buyer might like a pair of jeans in a store window so much he or she would be prepared to pay $50 when the price is in fact only $40. The buyer would then achieve a $10 consumer surplus. Of course, shopkeepers and other sellers would like to extract the buyer's consumer surplus, but it is difficult in many cases to charge each buyer a different price, even when they know the maximum buyers would pay. But let us return to factors of production and economic rent.

An obvious question to ask concerning economic rent is why firms don't form buyers' cartels to reduce competition in bidding for the factors of production. This might enable them to pay each individual worker or owner of land only that which they require to supply what they have to offer, that is, their reservation price or opportunity cost outside the cartel. In this way, those doing the hiring or renting—the baseball teams, automobile manufacturers, farmers, real estate developers, and so on—would keep economic rent for themselves rather than have it collected by the owners of the "resources." However, even if the required reservation price or opportunity cost were known, there is always an incentive to break a cartel. While it is better for baseball teams collectively to limit bidding between themselves by using a draft and sharing available talent without paying out the economic rents, for any individual team it pays to offer more than the collectively agreed price. After all, if the fans are prepared to pay to see a particular player it is worth hiring the player even if he must be paid above the wage set by the cartel.

Because of the incentive to break buyers' cartels, and because the law finds them undesirable—as in the case of the old baseball draft system—we do not see too many cartels succeeding in collecting economic rents. They are collected by the suppliers of factors of production rather than by the demanders of the factors.

Economists have been particularly fascinated by economic rent because it represents a marvelous tax base. This is because if the supply of a factor were rigidly fixed and had no alternative uses a tax would have no effect on final product prices or production; all of the effect flows from product prices to factor prices, not vice versa.

If we examine the views of non-economists on what determines wages and rents, we find some of these views consistent with economic thinking. We have already pointed out that the idea that people's incomes depend on their level of education agrees with the economist's way of thinking about MRPs and hence the demand for labor. The more education a worker has the higher the worker's MRP and the demand for labor and hence the higher the wages. The same goes for individuals' abilities if differential wages can be paid; more competent workers have higher MRPs and therefore also have higher wages. Similarly, the idea that union membership results in higher wages is seen to follow from the way market wages are determined, that is, by the supply and demand for labor; if unions can cause a reduced supply of workers they can increase market wages and the prices of what is produced.

An obvious limitation of the economic way of thinking about the determination of wages and other factor prices is that employers do not know the MRP of every factor they hire. Just imagine in a firm with 10,000 employers working out the contribution to firm revenue of yet another M.B.A. or accountant. Moreover, when product prices decline and MRPs also decline, firms do not fire their workers to the point where their MRPs again equal their wage rates; it could be expensive to rehire and retrain employees when conditions later improved. And even when firms do fire employees, they might well select those they do not like before those they do like, or they may be forced by unions to fire those without seniority even if this means keeping those with lower MRPs.

Another serious limitation of the economist's thinking about factor prices is that it does not provide any reason why the MRPs are what they are. This is an important shortcoming since we are often told that Western productivities are falling behind those in Japan and Hong Kong. Why is it that the Japanese ethos has outperformed our own? This is not a question that can properly be answered by positive economics, but it is perhaps more important to find the answer to this than to know that factor prices reflect opportunity costs.

Finally, we must recall that the concept of economic rent is very dangerous if we do not carefully identify the relevant market. The size of the rents owners of factors collect—such as workers who, of course, own their own labor services—depends on the market considered. For example, if we consider the market for professors of economics, only part of their wages are economic rents. This is because they can often find work in government and business. While some, like myself, would not shift for anything—at least not anything likely to be offered—others are living at the margin and sadly collect no rents at all. However, if we consider the market for economists, whether professors or professional economists, the rent is much higher because what else can they do?

CHAPTER 10

Thinking Selfishly

Free Enterprise and Economic Externalities

> The least pain in our little finger gives us more concern than the destruction of millions of our fellow-beings. WILLIAM HAZLITT
>
> Every individual ... generally neither intends to promote the public interest, nor knows how much he is promoting it.... But by pursuing his own interest he frequently promotes that of society more effectively than when he really intends to promote it. ADAM SMITH

PROPONENTS of the free enterprise, or *laissez-faire* philosophy believe that the selfish behavior of individuals, each setting out to maximize his or her own objectives, also maximizes social objectives. While plenty of economists can be found among those who support laissez-faire, not every economist has complete confidence that it is the best way to achieve social goals.

Those economists who advocate an unregulated marketplace argue that this allows consumers to dictate what is produced for them. According to this view, when consumers are willing to pay prices that exceed costs of production—more precisely, when marginal revenues exceed marginal costs—those items will be provided. Furthermore, increases in demand increase product prices making it profitable for suppliers to produce more. The consumer is therefore considered sovereign, with producers responding to consumer demands out of an incentive to make profits. Without the signals of prices provided by the free-market mechanism producers would not respond this way, and it would be necessary to find some way of rationing an insufficient supply.

Economists who favor government intervention, who of course differ in the extent of intervention they believe necessary, do not believe that consumers and producers necessarily do the best from a national perspective. The basis of their way of thinking is that the costs and benefits that individual consumers and producers take into account do not always include the costs and benefits of their actions for society in general. This is because the actions of individuals have ramifications that are external to themselves, which the economist refers to as *externalities,* or *spillovers.* Externalities are generally thought of as being negative, but careful consideration can uncover a number of positive spillover benefits of individual actions. This is true whether we are considering the actions of consumers or producers.

According to economic thinking, consumers compare the benefits of the different decisions they can make, which are measured as marginal utilities. In chapter 3 we explained how this can be used to maximize the total utility a consumer receives from a limited income. This involves consumers making decisions on, for example, what to purchase, so that per-dollar marginal utilities are equalized.

While this is the most convenient way of thinking about the factors affecting demand, it is not the best way of thinking about the effect of externalities. For this, we can use an approximation and think of consumers as deciding to buy a product if the marginal utility it provides exceeds the price the consumer must pay.

The comparison of marginal utility with the price or cost of products is an approximate way of thinking because, strictly speaking, we cannot define marginal utility with absolute units of measurement. However, it is common practice to make the cardinal assumption that we can measure benefits with *utils* and to proceed despite the fact that no one, not even a great economist, has ever encountered a util other than in the pages of economics books.

If utils did exist we could argue that as we consume more and more of a product the number of utils of benefit we get from consuming an extra unit of the product diminishes. If utils could be put in dollar terms and compared to product prices, it would pay to consume each product only until the point where the benefit in value of utils has dropped to the price or cost we pay for it—we stop where the benefit of the last unit consumed just equals the cost. After that point, the benefit would fall short of the cost and we should buy something else. Applying this to driving a car, we can claim that a person would drive until the benefit of an extra mile is reduced to the cost of driving an extra mile. The benefit comes in the form of getting to our desired destination and the cost, which is our *private cost,* is the gas, depreciation, time at the wheel, and wear and tear on the car.

While no other individuals are obvious benefactors of a person driving his or her own car there are others who bear costs. For example, the air pollution an individual produces is a cost to all who breathe it. Of course, the driver also breathes his or her own emissions, but this is a tiny consideration when he or she decides to drive; most of the emissions will be breathed by someone else. Similarly, when a person drives a car it adds to congestion, thereby slowing down other cars. In this case all the cost is borne by others and will not enter the driver's own calculation of the cost of driving an extra mile.

In the economist's jargon, pollution and congestion make the *social cost* of driving exceed the private cost we bear. This is a conventional negative externality. If we drive until our own private benefits equal our private costs, we will drive too much from the point of view of society; the social costs will exceed our private benefits which are the only benefits enjoyed by society. Only if we were forced to bear all the cost via some sort of tax per mile driven would we drive the correct amount from the social point of view. In such a situation, all the social costs would be *internalized,* so that private costs equal social costs.

Private costs are below social costs also in the case of socialized medicine. Even with limited, subsidized payments by the patient, the full social cost of medical care will exceed the private cost we bear leaving an incentive to consume too much. The incentive to overuse medical services is not overcome by having private medical insurance because an individual's insurance premium is not directly related to that individual's utilization rate. Therefore, privately funded Medicare via insurance faces some of the same problems as "free" medicine.

Another situation where social costs exceed private costs

is with the discarding of beverage bottles and cans. When an individual discards a soda bottle or beer can the ugly sight it causes will be suffered by others, not just the inconsiderate person. If the garbage is left in a neighborhood that the individual rarely visits, all the cost is borne by others.

A way of internalizing the social cost of discarding cans and bottles is to have deposits on containers that are refundable only when they are returned. Some U.S. states and many countries have realized this and mandated bottle and can deposits. Indeed, there is no reason why we should not have deposits on a much larger variety of products. We might then find fewer refrigerators, rusting automobiles, and other eyesores on the city streets and in the countryside. Alternatively, when we could identify the person who imposed the social cost by abandoning, for example, a car, we can charge him or her depending on where the car was abandoned. Leaving it in a lovely place could be far more expensive than discarding it in an industrial wasteland, providing an incentive for people to junk their cars in the correct place.

In general, we can think of criminal acts as situations where the social costs of people's actions exceed the private costs. When a mugger grabs an old lady's handbag the private cost is zero, provided the mugger is not caught. The mugger's private benefit is whatever is in the bag. If the probability of being caught is small, the expected private cost—the probability of being caught multiplied by the value of fore-gone opportunities while in prison—is likely to be smaller than the expected benefit. The higher the probability of being caught the higher the expected private cost and therefore, according to strict economic thinking, the lower the chance the crime will be committed. Similarly, the higher the foregone income while in prison the lower the incentive to commit the crime. This can explain why crime rates increase in times of heavy unemployment and why people with good legal prospects for earning an income are not found committing petty crimes.

The social cost of mugging includes the financial and emotional cost to the victim. Indeed, because the financial cost is just equal to the financial gain to the mugger, the financial costs and benefits cancel out and the overall effect is the emotional cost of being mugged. When the mugging also involves violence, a physical cost must be added to the emotional cost. There are then obvious grounds for internalizing the social costs by interning the criminal. Economists reason that the harsher the punishment the lower the *benefit to cost ratio* and the lower the incentive to choose a life of crime.

When an individual's actions do not affect others, economists tend to believe that the actions are not criminal. For example, prostitution that does not involve soliciting in the street and the use of "soft" drugs would be viewed, according to economic thinking, as involving no externalities and no case for criminal treatment. However, addictive drugs, which are invariably connected with organized crime, and overt prostitution, which offends innocent people, would be considered to involve externalities and would therefore require some method of internalizing social costs. Similarly, pornographic magazines that are discreetly handled are far more acceptable than pornography that is forced on others by being overtly displayed in magazine racks and shop windows.

THINKING SMALL

We discover that on these matters the thinking of economists is shared by many lawmakers who recognize externalities even if they do not all give them that title.

Some actions involve negative externalities only because the government is involved elsewhere. For example, the failure to wear automobile seatbelts when there is no public support for those who are maimed in accidents affects only those sufficiently stupid not to wear their belts. However, because the failure to wear seatbelts increases injury rates there are externalities where accident victims survive, and there are Medicare and welfare programs to pay their hospital bills. Others pay for the consequences of the individuals' decision. The economist is therefore not surprised to find societies with socialized medicine being the same societies imposing fines on those not wearing seatbelts.

Pollution and congestion from driving, frequent visits to doctors because fees are subsidized, junking pop bottles and cars, crime, and failing to wear seatbelts in a society with Medicare, are all examples of social cost exceeding private cost. However, we can also find examples where benefits to society, or *social benefits,* exceed the benefits we privately receive.

When people maintain their front lawn they provide an attractive sight to others in the neighborhood. In addition, by preventing dandelions from reaching the point of sending their seed into neighbors' gardens, an individual's own job of cutting the lawn imposes benefits on others in the form of fewer weeds in their lawns. When people upgrade their home they also upgrade their neighborhood. Any increase in value to neighbors' houses by the act of the individual is external to that individual, so we can expect upgrading to be below socially optimal amounts, that is, the correct amount from a neighborhood's perspective.

Another example where social benefits may exceed private benefits is with education. It has been extensively argued that everybody benefits from having other well-educated people with whom to interact. Not only does it provide benefits in terms of interaction, but education may be necessary for others to help us advance our standard of living and our enjoyment of that standard. How else are we to have the inventions that enhance our comfort, and the music and literature that help us enjoy our leisure? There are lots of spillovers from an educated population and this provides a rationale, in addition to "giving everybody a chance," for providing public education.

The extra social benefits of education might explain what on second thought could appear as inequitable. In particular, why is it that we spend more money to educate those who do well in school and college rather than on those who are having difficulties? On grounds of pure equity it might make more sense to put our resources into educating those who are struggling, rather than throwing billions of dollars into scholarships and fellowships for high achievers. However, if when they finish their education high achievers provide spinoffs that help us all, including those who found learning more difficult, we have a case for a subsidy. However, there is a case for such a subsidy for the high achievers only if the individuals who reward the rest of us do not receive this reward in the form of the salaries they earn.

When we consider production decisions, the economic way of thinking again involves a comparison of costs and benefits. The benefits are marginal revenues and the costs are marginal costs. We have seen that profit maximization involves selecting an output where the marginal revenue is equal to the marginal cost. When there are no externalities, this provides the best output for society since it involves producing more whenever the marginal revenue (social benefit) exceeds the marginal cost (social cost). However, when private and social costs and benefits differ profit-maximizing private decisions are suboptimal from a social perspective.

It is well known that power generation and steel manufacture pollute the air and sometimes pollute the waterways. Production of lumber defoliates forests causing soil erosion and the silting of rivers and streams. Side products of production of a number of manufactured goods include chemicals which are difficult to dispose of, noise in the neighborhood, effluents which may reach the water supply, acid rain in far away countries, and a variety of other definitely negative effects. However, these external costs are not considered in production decisions, and from a social perspective we find overproduction of goods with production externalities. When firms produce cars, newsprint, and so on at levels where their marginal revenues equal their private marginal costs, the social costs far exceed the social benefits. Therefore, production is at too high a level from the social point of view.

Internalization of externalities of production can be achieved by having taxes paid by manufacturers that reflect the cost borne by society. These must be levied on the volume and toxicity of pollutants generated by the firm, and distributed to those who suffer from pollution. If this is done, it becomes sensible to produce the amount that should be produced according to social considerations. This is because the private cost, including taxes based on pollutants generated, equals the social cost. This way of thinking is more flexible than the view of many non-economists that we should shut down the offending firms, which is equivalent to an infinite tax rate on pollution.

While economists tend to concentrate on the nasty spillovers/externalities of production, most notedly that of pollution, there are cases where there are positive externalities from productive activity. These come in the form of extra revenues or lower costs for other producers from a particular producer's activities.

An example of a positive externality can be found in the symbiotic relation between fruit growing and beekeeping. The more fruit trees a farmer plants the more fruit tree pollen there is for nearby bees to make honey. Similarly, the more bees there are the more pollination takes place, and the more fruit is likely to grow. An expansion in the size of each operation therefore increases the revenue of the other, a clear example of positive externalities.

Another example of positive externalities might be the benefits derived by export firms when their competition makes inroads into a new overseas market. This is because it may open the eyes of consumers to the competitor's product. When the initial Japanese automobile manufacturers penetrated the U.S. market consumers began to realize that Japanese cars were a viable alternative to domestically built and European vehicles in terms of quality, comfort, fuel efficiency, and so forth. They may not have bought the particular makes they saw but, for example, the more Toyotas people saw in the United States, the more Hondas would likely eventually be sold.

Where there are positive externalities firms tend to produce too little, the reverse of the case of negative externalities.

THINKING SMALL

This is because with positive externalities the marginal revenue faced by the firm is lower than the social marginal revenue where the social revenue includes benefits to other firms. Alternatively, the social marginal cost is lower than the private marginal cost. The firm's profit-maximizing level of production with its own marginal revenue equal to its marginal cost would be at a level where the social marginal revenue exceeds the social marginal cost. More should therefore be produced from a social perspective—adding more to benefits than costs—but it will not occur without internalization of external benefits. Why should the bee-keeper expand just to help the fruit farmer, or vice versa? Or why should any individual Japanese car firm work harder to sell cars abroad when some of the benefits accrue to others? We have here two cases for government subsidies, at least according to the thinking of economists who believe that positive externalities can have important effects.

When the government does intervene, whether it be to help exporters get a toehold in a new overseas market, to provide funds to beekeepers or fruit farmers, tuition for students, or socialized medicine, there is a hazard of excessive use of what is provided. For example, if the public faced a zero cost of Medicare it would be optimal for the public to use it until the marginal benefit is also zero. Similarly, if the cost of education is zero it pays to continue going to school until the private marginal benefit of further education is zero. This means that these services are used until their social benefit is small—because for each person the private benefit is zero—yet the cost of providing the services is most definitely not small. Therefore, from a social perspective we get overconsumption, the economist's euphemism for abuse.

Another problem with services provided to the public at a zero marginal cost is how to meet the social cost of providing them. How should we pay for education and Medicare? Some people argue that people should incur costs according to their ability to pay, and that this can be achieved with a tax on income or wealth. Other people argue that payment should be according to the benefits received. Those who receive the most from others being educated—the symphony goers and those who enjoy modern art and literature—should pay the most toward education. Similarly, only those firms involved in export trade should pay toward the subsidization of exporters via any export credits or export insurance the government provides.

While payment according to potential or actual benefits received from services provided by the government is a clever idea, it is usually impractical. The main reason is that it is too difficult to tell how much benefit a person or firm receives from a service. It might seem that this problem could be overcome by asking members of the public or firms how much benefit they receive, and taxing them accordingly. Unfortunately, respondents are likely to say that they receive no benefits. In this way they pay no part of the cost of providing services and yet continue to enjoy the benefits. This is the nature of all *public goods,* which are those we enjoy whether or not we pay for them ourselves; we all want the goods, but by saying we don't benefit from them in order to avoid paying we don't change their presence but do lower our personal costs.

A commonly cited example of a public good is law and order. Whether we personally pay or not, we are protected by the police and the courts. Yet, if we were to be charged according to our declared benefits we would all have an incentive to respond that we receive no benefits at all. Of course, if everybody does say that they receive no benefits the government, if it believes them, might not provide policing and courts, and people would all be worse off. However, it still would not be worthwhile for any individual to say he or she does receive benefits because that would not increase the chance that law and order would be provided by the government. What we have then is an example of a *fallacy of composition,* where each person acting individually does not behave in the way that is best for society.

It would appear that the fallacy of composition, coming as it does from the incentive to *free-ride* on the contributions made by others, can be overcome when the public sees through the veil. For instance, public television is a public good in that we can enjoy all we want while others pay, and yet our own contribution does not substantially increase the quality of programming: we would get the same quality whether or not we individually contribute. Yet some people do pay. Another instance where people pay for public goods despite the fact that almost all the benefits from their contributions accrues to others is medical research. While a large part is financed out of general revenue, there is still a substantial voluntary contribution from the public. We might be tempted to say that these examples demonstrate that people have civic responsibility or that they are for some unknown reason altruistic.

In some cases potential benefactors of public goods can be readily identified. The cost of running the United States Coast Guard could be charged to owners of commercial and pleasure boats, while television owners could be charged a license fee for public channels, as is done in the United Kingdom. Generally, however, everyone gains from public goods and we cannot meter the extent of their utilization. The most expedient way to pay is out of taxes and hope that utilization is related to the income base of the taxes. But this raises another question: How much of each different public good should the government provide?

If the government knows the benefits the public obtains from each public good it should provide each until the marginal social benefit received per dollar of providing them is the same for each. After all, this is the way private decisions should be made, that is, via equalization of marginal utilities per dollar. No other allocation could provide a better social benefit. However, because the public does not reveal the benefits it receives by the prices it pays or by its declarations, the government has to depend on its good sense of what the public would like to have, and this is not what conventional positive economic thinking can help the government decide.

Not only does the government face a problem of how to allocate spending best to achieve optimum social benefits, but it must decide the total amount it should spend on all of its services combined. This is a question concerning fiscal policy and is part of the economics of thinking big.

PART III

THINKING
BIG

*Macroeconomic
Reasoning*

CHAPTER 11

Thinking Definitively

Defining the Important Macroeconomic Terms

> English economists . . . have never set much store by
> matters of definition, and no doubt it is true that the
> nature of the pudding is best discovered by eating it.
> SIR DENIS H. ROBERTSON
>
> It is not the scarcity of money, but the scarcity of
> men and talents, which makes a state weak.
> VOLTAIRE

ECONOMISTS tend to put on a different thinking cap when tackling such big, national subjects as inflation, unemployment, national income, the balance of payments, and so on, than when they are considering individual consumers and firms. This is despite the fact that the national economy is made up of individual consumers and firms.

Firms and consumers are dealt with in the area of microeconomics where the central method of thinking involves marginal analysis and the resulting framework of supply and demand. However, national problems like inflation and unemployment are considered as macroeconomic problems and these have not typically been tackled with marginal analysis. Instead, economists have generally thought in terms of the flow of payments between consumers and firms, or in terms of the amount of money in circulation versus the output of goods and services that are available for purchase. Unfortunately, before we can appreciate the economists' way of thinking on macroeconomic or big questions, we must share their understanding of certain terms. Even such everyday terms as "money" and "output" are too imprecisely used by the ordinary person for clear economic thinking.

An economist thinks of *money* as being anything that is generally acceptable for making payments, whether these be for groceries, rent, auto repair services, or for one's services, that is, wages. It is general acceptability that matters because if others are likely to accept an item from you as a means of payment, you in turn are likely to accept that item from them. Many people have an idea of what they think is acceptable and what should therefore be considered as money—most commonly that which we hold in our wallets and pocketbooks. However, there are items that have served as money that would not occur on many non-economists' lists.

In North America, before the arrival of vast numbers of money-using Europeans, the Indians of the eastern and central part of the continent used wampum as a means of exchange. Wampum consisted of white and blue beads which were strung on bands and belts. On the West Coast, the more common medium was shells, gathered from the sea and beaches. Dentallium and abalone shells were tied into strings for everyday transactions. These media of exchange continued to circulate even after the arrival of

European immigrants. Contrary to the image depicted in many Western movies, not every trade took the form of barter via the direct exchange of such items as skins and blankets.

In the Yap Islands of the South Pacific tall monoliths of granite, which are not indigenous, have served as money for certain large transactions for centuries. Titles to the rocks are transferred in a way we might expect to see in the TV cartoon show "The Flintstones." The rocks are certainly not digestible or useful for building and have no apparent intrinsic value. They are acceptable as money because others have become used to accepting them. And that's all it takes.

Another example of an unusual money can be found in the former French colonies of North America. In the New France of the late 1600s, a shortage of silver coins developed that could not quickly be corrected because of the long sailing time from Europe. In the absence of a supply of suitable quality paper, the Intendant, or governor, decided to use playing cards. These were signed and then circulated as money, with a promise to redeem them for silver when the new coins arrived from France. The cards were cut into halves and again into quarters, with the quarters further cut on the diagonal for small change. This method of dividing up larger denominations was more straightforward than attempting division into tenths. The two halves of a quarter were referred to as "two bits."

How acceptability is the primary characteristic required of money can be found in more recent history. Well into the twentieth century central bankers of different countries settled at least some of their international transactions by paying in gold. Some of this gold was held for safekeeping in the vaults of the Federal Reserve Bank of New York. When the Bank of England wanted to pay the Bank of France, gold bars could be transferred from the Bank of England's room at the Fed to the room containing the gold of France. Then in the early 1970s, a weekly tabloid notable for its sensational headlines which trumpet at us on supermarket checkout lines, reported that the Fed's vaults were emptier than the bankers believed. Despite the paper's notoriety, it took a visit to the New York Fed's vaults by numerous U.S. Congress representatives to convince doubters that all was well.

What is revealing about this story is that it would not have mattered had the vaults been entirely empty, provided it was never discovered. The central bankers could have been satisfied indefinitely with their belief that the Fed was as good as gold. What matters with money is trust, which probably explains the words on every U.S. coin. Any medium in which there is trust in its acceptability by others will work as a money. This is true even if it has little or no intrinsic value like the Yap Island rocks, the playing cards of New France, the "belief" that gold was moving within the Fed's vaults, or the paper monies in circulation today. Of course, there is a problem of trust if central bankers who issue the paper money are not willing to limit the supply, as it is well known that they face no shortage of paper and ink.

For many years governments have recognized the importance of acceptability of their paper monies. They have therefore declared, as on every U.S. bill, that acceptance is mandatory "for all debts, public and private." The decree, or fiat, that a government's money is "legal tender" is usually made at the time that the intrinsic value is reduced below the stated value. This explains why all paper money and *debased* coins—coins that contain base metal—are known as *fiat money*. However, while a government can make it illegal not to accept fiat money, if it introduces it alongside money with the same face value but with higher intrinsic value, the fiat money will be all that is used. Why would anybody pay with money with intrinsic value if it will buy the same amount as the fiat money? Only the fiat money will circulate. The good money, like older coins with gold or silver content, will be hoarded.

The principle that "bad money drives out good" has become known as Gresham's Law, after the English economist who noted it, and it again reveals the key role of acceptability in the economist's thinking on money. It also shows that for monies of equal face value to simultaneously circulate they must not only be generally acceptable, but must also be equally acceptable.

What we have said so far will be part of just about every economist's thinking on money. Where economists do not all think alike is on the question of which assets in practice have general acceptability, and which should therefore be considered as part of the *supply of money*. In this, just about every economist will include coin and paper currency. Most will also include checking account balances as they are accepted for a vast variety of payments. But what about credit cards and bank balances that are not checkable, but which can quickly be moved into checkable accounts? Because the unused balances on credit cards and certain noncheckable deposits are perceived by those who have them as offering a degree of moneyness, many economists think about them as being part of the money supply. Others think of credit cards as credit, not as money, because eventually what is bought on cards must be paid for—in money. Funds that can be quickly transferred into checkable accounts clearly have a degree of liquidity and are close to money.

The fact that virtually every economist thinks that checking accounts are money, even if they cannot agree on other items, leads them to conclude that financial institutions like banks can make money. Non-economists tend to think differently, viewing banks not as makers of money, but as businesses that take in money from depositors (at relatively low interest rates) and lend it out again to borrowers (at higher interest rates). They therefore believe that while banks make profits from the interest rate *spread*—the lending rate minus borrowing rate—they do not make money. In the jargon of the economist, this popular non-economist's view emphasizes the role of banks and other financial institutions as *intermediaries* serving to redirect depositors' funds to those wishing to obtain loans. However, this intermediation directly influences the supply of money.

Thinking economically, when a bank makes loans it *monetizes debt*. That is, it converts *debt instruments* such as mortgages, government bonds, corporate bonds, or private consumer loans, into balances at the bank. The balances at the bank are money in that they are generally acceptable as a means of payment. Therefore, it is fundamental that we appreciate the extent to which banks can intermediate and so increase the money supply. We can do this by thinking about what happens if your bank is able to make you a car loan from $10,000 it has just received as a deposit.

Suppose your bank lends you $9,500 of the $10,000 it received, keeping $500 in "reserve." This will involve the bank crediting your account with $9,500 in return for your signing of a promissory note stating the schedule of interest and principal repayments, what happens if you don't pay, and a number of difficult to comprehend but important details. This note, a debt instrument, is an asset of the bank. Your credited account is money. The bank has therefore monetized your IOU to the tune of $9,500. What limits the ability of your bank to make loans from a given deposit, like the original $10,000, is that when you write a check against your augmented account, the bank must pay up. In particular, when the auto dealership where you buy your car deposits your check in its bank, your bank must transfer the full $9,500 to the dealer's bank. This is done via accounts both banks keep at a "clearing house," operated, for example, by the Federal Reserve System.

Your bank can grant loans only to the extent that it has funds in its account at the clearing house. Moreover, even if it has funds it cannot grant loans until its clearing account is completely empty because the authorities require banks to maintain *minimum reserves* which are related to the value of total customer deposits. This may be 5 percent of deposits and would explain why your bank held back $500 of its $10,000 deposit. However, while your bank can grant no more loans when it reaches the point of minimum required reserves, monies that it transfers to other banks allow them to grant more loans. So while each individual bank is severely limited to lending only what is deposited, and to a fraction of that, collectively the banks can lend a multiple of any initial increase in reserves. We can see this if we follow the $9,500 after you have spent it on the car and it has been deposited in the auto dealer's bank.

When the auto dealer's bank discovers its reserves increasing by the transfer of $9,500 into its account at the clearing house it will know that it can lend up to $9,025 of this. The balance of $475 must be held as a reserve against the $9,500 auto dealer's deposit (5 percent). When the $9,025 is loaned it is more than likely to be used to settle up with somebody keeping accounts at another bank. This next bank can then loan $8,573.75 of the $9,025 deposited, the next bank can loan 95 percent of $8,573.75, and so on. Hence, while each bank can loan only 95 percent of what it receives in deposits—explaining the view of non-economists and bankers that all banks do is intermediate—the original $10,000 bank deposit that enabled your bank to loan you $9,500 resulted in an increase in the money supply of $10,000 + $9,500 + $9,025 + $8,573.75 + $8,145.06 + ..., a series with an infinite number of terms which declines geometrically and has a total value approaching $200,000. While no individual bank appears to have made money, collectively there is little doubt that they have. And they have done it via each bank monetizing debt, which explains the economist's thinking that banks make money.

It is not only the bank account component of the supply of money that can be thought of as resulting from monetizing debt. Even the coins and currency we carry in our wallets and pocketbooks involve monetizing debt. Notes and coins are provided by central banks to the treasury branches of governments, in return for debt instruments such as Treasury bills and long-term bonds. We can therefore think of all money as being the result of converting debt instruments that are not themselves money into other instruments that are.

While economists tend to concentrate their thinking on the role of banks as makers of money, this does not mean that they would disagree with the view of non-economists that banks are businesses extracting a spread for intermediating between depositors and borrowers. Indeed, economists have even provided reasons why depositors do not try to circumvent the banks, lending directly to those currently borrowing from financial intermediaries.

Just think of what would be involved if instead of letting the financial intermediaries handle the flows of funds, you as a bank depositor had to find borrowers yourself. The problems in locating borrowers, writing up secure loan obligations, making sure that borrowers want the same maturity of loan you have in mind, that they want the amount you have to lend, and so on are tremendous. Moreover, you are unlikely individually to be able to pool a large number of loans so that your portfolio is diversified. Banks earn their spreads. They provide intermediation services, and their profits, determined in a competitive environment, are their rewards for these services. Therefore, the economist thinks of the interest rates we pay as being the result of what the banks must pay depositors. These payments are also needed to cover bank costs and hence ensure their survival. Non-economists do not invariably think the same way, often seeing banks as evil money lenders who extract as usurious an interest rate as they can. The economist knows it is not the bank's money that a bank lends. It is the money of its depositors, who also benefit when interest rates are very high.

What banks make for themselves from their provision of intermediation services is their income, or profit, and it comes from their spread. Income is fundamentally different from money. Income is what banks, other businesses, bank depositors, landlords, and you yourself, earn each month, calendar quarter, or year. Your income is paid in the form of money and is measured in money units, as dollars and cents. However, your income is not what you have in the form of coins, notes, and checking accounts at any given point in time. This is your money supply and it may amount to, for example, $215.78. On the other hand, your income is what you earn each month or year and may be, for example, $2,000 per month, or $24,000 per year.

The economist refers to money as having a *stock* dimension. Income is referred to as a *flow*. A stock has no time dimension. It is like the amount of water sitting in a sink that is measured as so many gallons and ounces, period, just as your money supply is so many dollars and cents, period. Income must be given a time dimension in order for it to have meaning. It is like water pouring out of a tap or a drain, so many gallons per minute or per hour. An income of $2,000 has a very different meaning if it is per month, rather than per year.

Because non-economists do not distinguish as carefully as economists between money and income they form sentences and arguments that make little sense economically. Consider the somewhat impertinent question, "How much money do you earn?" You could be asked, "How much money do you have?" but what you earn is your income. Saying that "banks make too much money" consequently has a very different meaning to economists than to non-economists. Indeed, because of the meaning of money to economists as something quite distinct from income, they believe that having vast amounts of money is unwise. Instead of having a large amount of our wealth in the form of money we should invest it in stocks, bonds, and so on, which, unlike money, yield a return. Furthermore, economists think inflation results from having too much money in circulation, but would very rarely argue that a nation can have too much income.

A nation's income, its national income, is the total amount earned by everyone in the nation. Just as our own incomes are flows, so is the national income. All forms of income are included in it, whether received as wages, salaries, interest, profits, or rents. Indeed, the fact that all forms of income are included in the national income allows us to calculate it in numerous ways. In particular, we obtain the same value from adding up the incomes received as we do from adding up the values of outputs produced, or amounts spent.

The different faces of national income are alike because firms pay their costs—wages, office equipment, and so on—out of the revenue received from selling their products. Everything that is left over from total revenue after meeting these costs are company profits. It therefore follows that the total revenues from what is sold are either distributed as incomes or retained as incomes, in the form of profits, by the owners of firms. It follows, then, that apart from some finer definitional details, the value of national income equals the value of the total sales in the nation.

The value of goods and services sold is referred to as *gross national expenditures,* or *GNE.* It should be apparent that if everything produced is also sold, then the GNE is the same as the value of production in the nation, which is known as the *gross national product,* or *GNP.* Actually, even if some goods are produced and not sold it has little effect on this important identity. The economist thinks of unsold goods as *inventory accumulation* and considers this to be an investment, and therefore part of the spending of companies. Therefore, inventories are included in expenditures, preserving the equality between the GNE and GNP.

When we think of the gross national product, gross national income or expenditures, we can think of them in two different forms. The two forms of the GNP are referred to as the *nominal GNP* and the *real GNP*.

Nominal GNP is the value of all the goods and services produced, including any effects of price increases, that is, inflation. It is the total value of everything produced in the nation and is obtained by adding the dollar value of new cars, new homes, loaves of bread, heads of lettuce, haircuts, and every other thing that is produced. All are valued at the prices at which they are sold. We have to be careful not to include anything twice, such as the steel used in making cars as well as the cars themselves, or the wood used in making furniture as well as the furniture, so as to avoid *double counting.*

The problem with the nominal GNP as a measure of the nation's health is that if every final output were to double in price, so would the GNP. The GNP would also double if the nation produced twice as many cars, haircuts, and so on, with these sold at their old prices. A doubling of output is far more healthy than the same output costing twice as much. This is why we need to define the real GNP.

Real GNP is a measure of the volume, or quantity of output, rather than the current market value of that output. We can present the definition of real GNP with a straightforward example.

Suppose that a nation produces a universally useful substance that can be eaten, worn, burned as fuel, used for constructing houses, and so on. Let's call this incredible product "Flexiput." Say that in 1984 the total national output of Flexiput was 5,000 tons, with each ton selling for

$1. The nominal GNP would be $5,000, which is the total value of all goods and services—in this case Flexiput—produced during this particular year.

Suppose that in the following year, 1985, output of Flexiput increases to 5,200 tons, and that for some reason called inflation the price rises to $1.10 per ton. The nominal GNP is $1.10 × $5,200 = $5,720, which is the value of 5,200 tons of Flexiput at $1.10 per ton. However, the real GNP is $5,200 *when measured in 1984 prices*. The way we come up with the real GNP is to value the current year's—that is, 1985's—output of 5,200 tons, at the base period's—that is, 1984's—price of $1 per ton. This avoids the influence of inflation in valuing national output. We observe that in general, real GNP is defined as the current output valued in the prices of a particular base period.

It is worthwhile noticing that by comparing the real GNP and the nominal GNP we can get a measure of inflation. Dividing the nominal GNP by the real GNP: $5,720 ÷ $5,200 = 1.10, in which .10, the increase in price per Flexiput ton in 1985, is 10 percent in decimals. This tells us that prices have risen 10 percent between 1984 and 1985. Put differently, 10 percent of the increase in nominal GNP was because of prices. In case this isn't clear let us extend the example.

Suppose that in 1986 the output of Flexiput increases to 5,500 tons, and the price also rises further to $1.25 per ton. Nominal GNP becomes $1.25 × 5,500 = $6,875. Real GNP in 1984 prices—when the price of Flexiput was $1—is 5,500 × $1 = $5,500. Taking the ratio of nominal to real GNP gives $6,875 ÷ $5,500 = 1.25. This tells us that the accumulated inflation between 1984 and 1986 is 25 percent.

The measure of inflation formed by comparing nominal

and real GNP is known as the *GNP deflator*. The GNP deflator covers all goods and services produced by the nation because the GNP is the value of all final outputs. Therefore, it provides a more accurate view of overall inflation than the more commonly cited *Consumer Price Index,* or *CPI*. The CPI, which concentrates on the basket of goods bought by a typical urban consumer, does not include a large part of what is produced in the way of industrial equipment, government services, and so on, which the consumer does not purchase. While the CPI may be useful for discovering what has happened to the buying power of the typical consumer, there are situations where the GNP deflator provides a better picture of overall inflation.

You may be wondering why we don't measure inflation directly in terms of the price of Flexiput and the real GNP in terms of the tons of Flexiput produced. We could then say that prices were up by 10 percent in 1984 and 15 percent in 1985, and also that the real GNP increased from 5,000 to 5,200 tons between 1984 and 1985, and from 5,200 to 5,500 tons between 1985 and 1986, with no need to value Flexiput in base period prices. Well, you are thinking well, but recall that the ability to measure inflation or the real GNP in terms of the prices or the output of Flexiput is only because we have no other outputs in our example. In the real world, we have a nominal GNP made up of new cars, new houses, tubes of toothpaste, cavities filled, letters delivered by the mail service, and so forth. We cannot add the prices or number of cars to the cost of mailing or number of letters delivered and come up with meaningful numbers; it's like adding apples and oranges, only worse. To obtain the GNP we have to add the dollar values of all the outputs rather than quantities produced and from this obtain inflation. The important difference is that the nominal GNP uses the current year's prices for the evaluation, and the real GNP uses those of a base period. Consequently, the nominal GNP is often called the *current dollar national product,* and the real GNP is called the *constant dollar national product.*

To obtain the real national income, as opposed to the real national product, we cannot value the incomes in a base year's prices because incomes are not outputs and do not have prices. What we do instead is divide the national income, which is the sum of all current dollar incomes, by the deflator obtained from the nominal and real national product. If the national product has risen, say, 25 percent due to inflation, we can expect incomes to have risen 25 percent too, because the national income and national product are just different sides of the pie. Consequently, we define the real national income (as well as the real national expenditure) as the current dollar value divided by the GNP deflator. In this way we preserve the equivalence of the income, product, and expenditure forms of the nation's performance, whether measured in nominal or in real terms.

Living standards depend on the volume of output, not on its value. It therefore goes without saying that as far as our standard of living is concerned, nationally as it is individually, what matters is real income and real product. Sound economic thinking must recognize this basic fact. This is not to say that it is not already recognized by a vast number of people who have not had an economics education. However, it is not difficult to lose sight of the distinction between real and nominal income when it appears in subtle forms.

Because it is only the volume of output that determines

the standard of living, it is unlikely to be immediately affected by the money supply. We could have billions of dollar bills handed to all of us without making us wealthy. Similarly, we could all take a hefty drop in wages and salaries without making us poorer. This is because if we produce as much as before, the product is the same, and so is real income. However, the possibility that people might spend more after receiving dollar bills, and that they might balk at declining wages, makes nominal values potentially more than a veil.

Even if we take care to compute the real GNP or real national income to judge standards of living, we must be extremely careful in comparing the resulting statistics for different countries. Comparing the incomes of nations, even if the incomes are real and adjusted for the number of people sharing them, is fraught with difficulty. For example, national income statistics do not include services done in the home. A society where a family member takes care of the children will therefore appear poorer than a society where children are in commercial daycare centers. Indeed, if parents exchange children during the day and pay each other the GNP would increase. A man marrying his housekeeper will similarly lower the measured GNP.

Another problem in comparing national incomes is that while GNP includes imputed services from homes, it doesn't include services provided by other durables like cars, books, refrigerators, public treasures like sculpture and art, antique furnishings, and so forth. A country where people enjoy marvelous luxuries, such as sculpture gardens, that were provided in the past will appear poorer than if it has no treasures and everything must be currently produced.

National incomes are also not related to "need." For

example, in the Northern United States and Canada a substantial portion of income is devoted to keeping warm and communicating over vast distances. The fact that real income per capita is much higher than some warm Caribbean islands where communications problems are minimal overstates the real differences in living standards.

The treatment of government in national income also contributes to difficulties in comparisons. Invariably, payments to government employees are added to the private product to compute the GNP even though this may involve what we have previously referred to as double counting. Government work promoting exports may already be valued in the exports so that if we add the payment to government employees to the value of output we double count. As different countries have different roles fulfilled by government, comparisons can be difficult.

There are numerous other problems. We never value leisure, for example, so that countries with short work weeks look poorer than we might want to consider them. Another problem involves the exclusion of such "outputs" as pollution and crime, which raise real GNP by increasing cleanup and policing expenses, but which are "bads" rather than goods. Real income figures might also be misleading if lining-up times differ greatly between nations. (In the Soviet Union, the average time spent waiting in lines reached 200 hours per person per annum by 1983.) Production of weapons of destruction is also included along with the output of grain and ice cream, despite a growing disutility of frightened citizens, and so forth.

While comparison of real GNP in different years for the same nation does not present such extreme problems as comparison of real GNPs of different nations we must still exercise caution. Dollars and cents are a narrow focus of what matters to many people. High incomes and high monetary living standards can come at the cost of physical and mental suffering, family disintegration, and other hardships. Because changes from year to year in such conditions are likely to be small, short-term comparisons remain useful. However, other measures of well being might be appropriate for comparing over longer intervals.

CHAPTER 12

Circular Reasoning

The Circular Flow of Income

> Society is composed of two great classes: those who
> have more dinners than appetites and those who
> have more appetites than dinners.
>
> SEBASTIEN R. N. CHAMFORT

> Let us all be happy and live within our means, even
> if we have to borrow the money to do it with.
>
> ARTEMUS WARD

IF THERE ARE any obviously economic matters on
which non-economists hold opinions these must certainly
include inflation and unemployment. Popular opinions
cover just about every shade of political belief, but despite
the broad following some of them enjoy, they rarely agree
with the thinking of economists.

A common view of inflation that, like currents in a
river, surface here and there depending on the course of
events, is that it is caused by excessive wage demands by
unions. By threatening work stoppages and other restrictive
practices, unions are perceived as forcing businessmen to
charge more to cover costs and survive. For quite obvious
reasons this line of argument is known as the *cost-push*
explanation of inflation. We do not need to display the

political colors of those with perceptions like this, other than to say that unions make them see Red. Nor need we describe the politics of those taking the antithetical position.

When union members and others who lean left think of inflation, the blame is generally placed on businessmen. The problem, it is often claimed, is that businessmen are always trying to squeeze an extra buck from the consumer. This forces up prices of what workers must buy causing them to demand higher wages. Worst of all businesses, according to this view, are the monopolies that can get away with "unfair" prices. Not surprisingly, because this requires strong demand to support the higher prices, it is known as the *demand-pull* explanation of inflation.

When people run out of culprits evident in their own environment they tend to look in other camps. Among the more obvious candidates who live in very fine camps indeed are the members of OPEC, who by forming a cartel, cost us hundreds of billions of petrodollars. Basing inflation on a cartel like OPEC involves a special case of the argument that inflation is the result of monopoly power. But as we shall see, this argument does not hold water—or oil. Economists can perceive OPEC as the spark that ignited a round of inflation, but even with all its oil and gas it could not continually flame the fire itself.

Also present on many non-economists' shortlists of candidates for the most powerful force behind inflation are governments. By spending in excess of what they raise in taxes, it is felt that they have forced up the prices of what we too must purchase.

When it comes to the question of unemployment, non-economists frequently think in terms of people being displaced by machines. Situations are cited where labor-saving technologies have done away with the need for people. The idea has broad appeal despite the general awareness of the fact that more are working today than before the nineteenth-century Industrial Revolution, despite its introduction of a vast array of machines. The appeal has also not been substantially affected by the fact that in a competitive international marketplace, if any individual country or company failed to use the latest available technologies they would surely end up with fewer jobs.

Competition from abroad, whether inspired by foreign technological advances or not, is another often cited source of unemployment. By being willing to work hard and long for little reward, cheap foreign labor is seen as forcing people out of jobs.

Even in a purely domestic or *closed* context, unemployment is sometimes viewed as the result of high wages. These are perceived as lowering demand for workers and are blamed on unions or the overly generous wages in government, which gets a large part of the blame for causing unemployment. Depending on the politics of those making accusations, the cause is either too much government spending or too little, with both sides convinced their viewpoint is based on the soundest of evidence.

It is also not uncommon to hear that unemployment is the result of a large number of people entering the workforce. At different times the blame has been placed on working wives, baby-boom children getting out of school or college, new immigrants, or too many people moving to the Sun Belt or West Coast.

Despite the apparent logic and broad appeal of some of these commonly heard opinions about inflation and unemployment, they are not the stuff of economic thinking.

THINKING BIG

Economists use positive thinking. Most of the common opinions, however, are just that—opinions—and are normative, that is, based on subjective reasoning. This does not mean that economists would necessarily disagree that unions or OPEC have caused inflation, or that unemployment is caused by too high wages or government policy. Instead the economist prefers to reach such conclusions out of an objective model.

Some models can be used to generate conclusions that correspond to the everyday opinions we have cited, but at some stage they usually require the application of assumptions about how politicians behave. Alternatively, we need to make political actions endogenous. For example, cost-push inflation—that caused by union demands—turns out to depend on *accommodation* by the government to each successively higher level of prices. Accommodation means the creation of the extra money required to allow people to make the higher payments. Indeed, it is the fact that political dimensions cannot be ignored that explains why economics is frequently referred to as political economy.

Just as in politics, where wise men facing the same set of facts and similar experiences reach very different conclusions, so it is in economics. Some schools of thought draw conclusions that seem quite unrelated to the popular opinions we have cited. Monetarists argue that oil price increases are inflationary only if they are accommodated via monetary expansion. Other schools of thought draw conclusions that correspond quite closely to the everyday opinions we have cited here. Such a school is the Keynesians'.

Keynesians base their thinking on the ideas of the great British economist John Maynard Keynes, many of which are found in his extensively read *General Theory of Employment, Interest, and Money,* published in 1936. The central feature of Keynesian thinking is the *circular flow of income.* This refers to the flow of payments from firms to consumers as wages, interest, profits, and rent, and from consumers to firms, as consumers buy the firms' products. If the flows from firms to consumers and from consumers to firms are of equal magnitude, Keynesians believe the flows can continue without changing. It would be rather like the water leaving a fountain being all pumped back in again. The fountain could continue without drying up or overflowing provided that within the circular flow any leakages are matched by new injections.

Keynesians explain inflation and unemployment by identifying the leaks and injections in the circular flow of income. The leaks are those of savings, taxes, and imports. These draw funds out of the circular flow between firms and consumers in a nation and reduce the level in the system. Savings and taxes represent parts of the incomes paid by firms which consumers do not spend on the products of firms, while imports mean leakages overseas. If these were the only forces at work they would soon empty the system. However, counterbalancing the leakages from the circular flow of income are injections of funds caused by business investment, government spending, and exports.

Business investment involves spending on plant expansion or capital equipment and the accumulation of inventory. This spending adds to that of consumption thereby augmenting the flow of income. The funds injected in the form of business investment are the other side of the recycled funds withdrawn by savers, because when firms invest in plant expansion or new equipment they must either use their own savings or somebody else's savings. This link between savings and investment can be seen if we think about how a firm can finance capital expenditures.

If the firm does not have its own savings from previously retained earnings it can borrow (incur debt) or sell new shares (raise equity). Borrowing can be from a bank or from the public. If it is from a bank, the bank is in effect lending funds it has gathered from savers who have placed them on deposit. Hence the bank merely intermediates between the savers and investors. If the borrowing is from the public by selling bonds, the bonds are directly bought out of peoples' savings. The same is true if the public uses its savings to buy shares. Rather than involve the banks, the bond or stock sales are intermediated by recognized brokers, who are therefore also financial intermediaries. So we can see that when a firm injects spending into the circular flow of income it either uses its own savings or somebody else's savings, and it is the intermediaries who serve as conduits between the savers and investors.

Keynesians argue that *ceteris paribus* or other things being equal, if the amount injected as investment equals the amount withdrawn as savings, the circular flow of income is balanced; the flows can continue unabated. However, if the amount firms want to invest happens to exceed the amount people want to save, in other words, if desired injections exceed desired withdrawals, the system may overflow. Similarly, if desired savings happen to exceed desired investment the flow may run dry, just as larger leakages than injections of water will empty a fountain.

Because desired investment versus desired savings is so important to Keynesian thinking, Keynesians have devoted a considerable amount of attention to why savings and investment can differ. They believe they have uncovered an important reason for desired savings to exceed desired investment during times of heavy unemployment.

Keynesians think that desired savings and investment are kept in line by movements in interest rates. It is argued that as interest rates fall businessmen want to invest more. This is because it is cheaper to borrow when they have no savings themselves, and they forgo lower interest earnings if they use their own savings. (In the economist's jargon, the opportunity cost of using their own savings to pay for expansion is lower when interest rates are lower.) In addition to the stimulation of investment caused by declining interest rates, lower rates also reduce savings. This is because at lower interest rates, savers would rather spend and enjoy themselves than put funds away. (Again, in the ubiquitous jargon, the opportunity cost of people spending rather than saving is lower at lower interest rates.)

The effect of lower interest rates on desired investment and desired savings is what in general causes the two to be equal. For example, if for a moment desired savings exceeded desired investment, tending to decrease the flow of income, the excess of savings would tend to lower interest rates. This would stimulate desired investment, lower desired savings, and thereby eliminate the excess of savings over investment. Similarly, if for a moment the amount saved fell short of desired investment, interest rates would increase. This would raise savings, lower investment, and restore balance, that is, remove the deficiency of desired savings versus desired investment.

Keynesians believe that if interest rates could always do their job there would never be a gap between savings and investment. The circular flow of income could continue unabated and continue around its steady upward trend. However, they argue that if for some reason we reached the point of very low interest rates—perhaps because we ran out of good investment opportunities—the *equilibrating mechanism* might falter.

In order to appreciate the Keynesians' fear of a faltering equilibrating mechanism suppose that at the going interest rate desired savings exceed desired investment. Then interest rates would have to fall lower to get them equal again—by lowering savings and increasing investment. But there is a limit to how low interest rates can fall because they cannot become negative; people always have the option of holding money that offers a zero interest yield. According to Keynesian thinking, even at zero interest rates, desired savings (a withdrawal), could exceed desired investment (an injection). The circular flow of income would therefore decline and interest rates could not stop the fall.

Even in the sorry state of a failure of the interest rate equilibrating mechanism, the economy would reach a bottom because the nation's savings depend not only on interest rates but also on national income. As national income falls people have lower incomes from which to save, so savings also fall. Consequently, if the economy went into a nose dive because savings exceeded investment even at a zero interest rate, savings would fall and eventually equal investment. (This also requires that investment does not decline as rapidly as savings with national income.) Keynesians believe that this is what happened in the Great Depression of 1929–33, which just preceded the development of Keynes's theory. Desired savings exceeded desired investment at interest rates that were effectively zero (rates were as low as a half percent on some government securities).

This prompted Keynes to argue that some way must be found to overcome such situations where withdrawals exceed injections at all (positive) interest rates.

Keynes and his followers found their solution in another pair of withdrawals and injections, those of taxes and government spending. Taxes, as we have said, are withdrawals from the flow of income while government spending is obviously an injection. Keynes said that if private withdrawals were larger than private desired injections then the government should inject more in spending than it withdraws in taxes, that is, the government should run a deficit. The net injections would offset the net desired private withdrawals, keeping the circular flow steady.

The Keynesian way of thinking can be characterized as fiscal intervention to maintain a steady flow of income. There is a lot of intuitive appeal to this argument, which is particularly valid if the economy runs into what Keynes described as the *paradox of thrift*.

Keynes observed that when the economy begins to falter and show signs of recession the natural reaction of the public is to increase savings. After all, their accumulated savings—part of their wealth—might be all they have to live on if their dire predictions are correct. However, when the economy does begin to falter we need the public to reduce their withdrawals, that is, their savings, not increase them. Hence what is the best way for each person to react in times of a faltering economy is the worst for the nation, an unfortunate paradox. (It is also a further example of a fallacy of composition as that faced with public goods, explained in chapter 10.) That is why Keynes was so emphatic on interventionist *fiscal policy,* the policy of managing government deficits to stabilize the economy. He felt that the government should

187

offset imbalances present in the private sector.

The Keynesian's explanation of inflation is the reverse of their view about unemployment. Inflation results when injections, such as investment and government spending, exceed withdrawals, such as savings and taxes. However, because Keynes himself was writing at a time when inflation was hardly the problem—prices fell by over 30 percent during the Great Depression—the *General Theory* and much subsequent Keynesian literature had little to say about inflation. Similarly, there is not much in Keynesian thinking on another potential cause of withdrawals differing from injections, namely that resulting from imports and exports.

When people spend their income on imports, their spending is withdrawn from their own country's circular flow of income. Offsetting this withdrawal are exports, which are an injection. If a country has a deficit in its balance of trade, which means that it is importing more than it is exporting, withdrawals will exceed injections, lowering the circular flow of income. An important question is, therefore, whether there is an equilibrating mechanism analogous to that of interest rates in the case of savings and investment. And if there is a mechanism, it is important to discover whether there are circumstances where it might break down.

The most immediate mechanism tending to restore equality between imports and exports is the exchange rate. When a country has a trade deficit, its residents are spending more abroad than they receive from abroad. This means that more of the country's money is being supplied to the foreign exchange market (via importing) than is being demanded (via exporting). As is generally the case when supply exceeds demand, the price falls, which in this case means the international value of the currency should fall. For example, if the United States has a trade deficit, then, *ceteris paribus,* it should make the U.S. dollar fall in value in terms of British pounds, German marks, and so on. This is the basis of the automatic adjustment mechanism. The cheaper currency makes the country's exports cheaper and also means an increase in import prices. This stimulates exports, reduces imports, and should eventually eliminate the deficit.

If we had freely moving exchange rates—*flexible rates*—and everything else were equal, the adjustment would be complete. Exports would balance with imports; these withdrawals and injections would be equal. However, we have not always had flexible exchange rates and everything else is not equal. Exchange rates are changed not only by imports and exports, but by flows of money for investments in stocks, bonds, and so on. Hence withdrawals via imports will not necessarily equal injections via exports, even with flexible exchange rates, and the circular flow of income can be affected.

As we have said, Keynesian thinking has not put much emphasis on the international side of the circular flow problem. However, Keynesian thinking that has occurred follows the same lines as with savings and investment. For example, it is said that if there is a balance of trade deficit with imports (a withdrawal) exceeding exports (an injection), the circular flow of income will decline until this reduces imports sufficiently to restore balance. This happens because, as with consumption of domestically produced goods, imports depend on income. The government can prevent the decline in income with injections (via government spending) exceeding withdrawals (via taxes).

We have so far explained only how the discretionary application of fiscal policy can prevent changes in the flow of income coming from differences between private withdrawals and injections. In reality, the government may itself be the cause of imbalance because there is no requirement that it balance its spending and taxes when the private withdrawals and injections are balanced. Indeed, the government almost invariably seems to have a fiscal deficit resulting in larger injections than withdrawals even when there are also larger injections than withdrawals in the private sector. In such a situation the government is adding to the overflow of the circular flow of income. Far from being the agent of balance, the government itself is tipping the scales.

According to Keynesian thinking, net injections, whether caused by government or not, are not always inflationary. Having injections exceed withdrawals is inflationary only if the economy is operating at or above capacity. It is only then that a higher circular flow of income cannot be of real income. Similarly, net withdrawals will not always cause unemployment. However, whether they will depends not only on the degree of capacity utilization, but on the flexibility of wages.

Keynes and his followers realized that as the circular flow of income declines people can remain employed, provided they accept lower wages. Then the flow of income can be smaller, not because some people have zero incomes, but rather because the dollar amounts per person are smaller. If this is what happens, real income is unchanged. After all, if everybody continues to work even at lower dollar wages, the real output, which is the result of the number working and their effort, should not be affected. However, Keynes thought that a reduction only in wages and not in real income was highly unlikely. Keynes realized that wages and prices are relatively inflexible or "sticky" downward, requiring a serious economic recession before they are reduced. In the interim, people are fired or laid off. Hence, Keynes thought that when withdrawals exceed injections—because savings plus taxes plus imports exceed investment plus government spending plus exports—unemployment increases. However, this is not only the result of the reduction in the circular flow of income, but also of the inflexible wages.

Yet another thread of Keynesian thinking concerns the effect, or lack of effect, of increasing the money supply in order to prevent a decline in the circular flow of income when withdrawals exceed injections. Keynesians argue that putting more money—as defined in the previous chapter—into the economy will not stimulate demand. The reasoning is based on the Keynesians' view of the demand for money, which they refer to as the *liquidity preference function*. This is the demand for currency, checking accounts, and so on, which is limited because people prefer to have most of their wealth in earning assets.

Keynesians believe that at the low interest rates seen during a very severe recession, people hold on to any increase in the supply of money. Why invest it to earn interest if the interest rates are so low? Moreover, why put the money into bonds whose prices fall as interest rates increase from their extraordinary low levels. Consequently, Keynesians believe that during recessions increases in the supply of money will be matched by increases in the demand for money, making monetary policy ineffective. It is on this point that the other major school of economic thought, the Monetarists, think very differently.

CHAPTER 13

Fast Thinking

The Quantity and Velocity of Circulation of Money

> A greenback is a familiar form of paper money that's built more for speed than endurance.   EVAN ESAR

> The government is the only organization that can run a deficit and yet still make money.
> Anonymous

MONETARISTS think about prices in general in the same way they think about individual prices, that is, in terms of supply and demand. However, when they are thinking about the overall level of prices they are more concerned with the supply and demand for money than they are with the supply and demand for the products money buys.

In a nutshell, Monetarists argue that if the central bank allows an increase in the supply of money that exceeds the demand for money, this will lower the buying power, or value, of money. A lower buying power for money means that it does not go as far, that is, prices are higher. But what is it that determines the supply and demand for money? After all, it might seem odd to think at all in terms of the demand for money.

The supply of money has already been defined, and we have established that it is the generally accepted means of exchange, consisting of banknotes, checking accounts at banks, and other similar items. We also made it clear that the supply of money is primarily determined by the central bank, which controls both the total amount of bank reserves and the required fractional reserve ratio.

While the supply of money is determined by the central bank, the demand for money is determined by the public. But just in case you think the public has an infinite demand for money, recall that money is not income. Money is the stuff we hold to make purchases, and if we hold more of it we give up the chance to earn interest and dividends which can be earned by investing it in other assets. Therefore, money involves an opportunity cost, and the demand is finite. For example, if instead of holding money you could buy a bond offering 10 percent interest, you give up ten cents per year on each dollar of money you hold, which of course means each dollar you do decide to hold as money is providing you with at least ten cents worth of services per annum, or you wouldn't hold it.

What money provides is convenience. This is because if you see something you wish to purchase, you can pay for it immediately. If you did not hold money, and instead kept your wealth exclusively in the stock market or some interest-bearing security, in order to make a purchase you would have to sell the stock or the security to convert it into money. This would involve brokerage charges. Furthermore, you would not be sure ahead of time how much you would receive for the stock or security because stock and bond prices have a habit of fluctuating.

THINKING BIG

Monetarists believe that people who have higher incomes like to have more convenience both in terms of what they buy and the amount of money they hold. They therefore believe that the demand for money is directly and positively related to people's incomes. In more carefully stated versions, income is calculated as an average over a long period. For example, the person earning $20,000 per year might like to keep, that is, demand, $4,000 in money. If the same person were to face a permanent increase in income to $25,000, he or she might wish to hold $5,000 of money.

Of course, the amount of money an individual actually holds will go up and down as income comes in and expenditures drain money out, so we think of average money holdings and average income. However, when we add up everyone's incomes and money holdings the deviations from averages tend to cancel out, and the relation between the desired aggregate of money demanded and the national income can reasonably be assumed to be steady.

Monetarists go a step further than saying that there is a steady link between the demand for money and national income. They also say that if the national income or expenditures were, for instance, to double, people would want to hold approximately twice as much money. Their rationale is that if nominal expenditures doubled, either because prices or real expenditures doubled or a combination of both, people would need twice as much money for the same convenience. If a person leaves the house with an average of $20 when the bus ride costs $1, the newspaper fifty cents, and so on, and then the bus ride goes to $2 and the newspaper to $1, the person would need to leave with $40 to retain the same real buying power for the day and therefore the same convenience.

With the supply of money being determined by the central bank, and the demand for money being determined by national income and in proportion to that income, the Monetarist has a tidy way of thinking about inflation. It goes like this:

Suppose that people start out holding the amount of money they want to hold, and that the money supply is then increased by 10 percent. The public will have 10 percent more money than they want to hold and therefore will be out of equilibrium. In order to reduce their monetary holdings to the desired amount, they will invest the money in, say, bonds, or use it to buy goods they want. However, money is like the potato in the game of Hot Potato. An individual can hand it to somebody else, but it doesn't cease to exist.

As the public tries to get rid of the extra 10 percent supply of money by buying bonds and goods, it will cause certain changes. The attempt to get rid of money by buying bonds will not get rid of the money, but it will raise bond prices. As we explained in chapter 5, as the price of bonds goes up, because the outstanding bonds offer a given coupon, the yield declines. While a $1,000 bond paying coupons of $50 per year yields 5 percent, if the price of the bond were to increase to $1,500 the $50 coupons would represent a yield of only 3.3 percent.

As interest rates decline from the increase in the money supply this may increase the quantity of money demanded because it lowers the opportunity cost of holding money. However, the Monetarist believes that interest rates have only a minor effect on money demand; the increase in demand for money from the drop in interest rates is not likely to restore the equality of supply and demand.

The Monetarist turns attention to the other way people try to get rid of extra money, that is, by buying goods. By directly buying extra goods in an attempt to reduce the amount of money held to the desired level, the goods' prices are likely to increase. This is especially probable if the economy is running at capacity and therefore cannot produce more. Higher prices raise nominal income and expenditures, and thereby raise the demand for money. Given the view of the Monetarist, the demand for money will move up the same percentage as the increase in prices brought about by the extra spending.

Here then is the Monetarists' theory of inflation, which is called the *Quantity Theory of Money*. If we start from an equilibrium where the supply and demand for money are equal, and then the money supply is increased by 10 percent, it will lower interest rates and raise prices. The effect of the decrease in interest rates is by assumption small, but the effect of higher prices and hence higher nominal national income is to raise the demand for money, by assumption, in the same proportion as income. If the effect of lower interest rates is so small that we need not consider it, the only way that the demand for money can move up toward the higher supply is via the increase in prices and national expenditures. Indeed, the increase in prices and expenditure is the economy's equilibrating mechanism.

How much will prices increase from the 10 percent increase in the money supply? The answer is that they will increase by 10 percent—that is, in exact proportion to the increased money supply. The reason is that the demand for money goes up and down in the same proportion as national expenditures, at least according to the assumptions of the Monetarists. It follows that it is only when national income and expenditures have risen by 10 percent that money demand will be 10 percent higher, hence matching the increase in the money supply. However, if real GNP is already at capacity, all of the 10 percent increase must be in prices.

The Monetarists' conclusion about inflation has been reached in this example, and this is that inflation is caused by too much money chasing too few goods. If the money supply is increased 10 percent in each year, *ceteris paribus* the annual inflation rate should be 10 percent. The conclusion depends on the assumptions that quantitative effects of interest rates and national income are as we described. By using the assumption that declining interest rates have little effect on money demand, and the assumption that money demand moves in proportion to national expenditures, we get prices increasing in proportion to the money supply, if we begin at full employment. As we mentioned at the end of the previous chapter, Keynesians reach a different conclusion.

An increase in prices caused by increasing the money supply or anything else is called inflation only while prices are increasing. It follows that an increase in the money supply to a new level without further increases does not cause inflation as it is generally understood. This is because prices should cease increasing when they have risen in line with the money supply. For example, when the money supply is increased by 10 percent and prices are 10 percent higher, there is no reason for inflation to continue. Indeed, if the money supply increase took place on a particular day, and if the price adjustment occurred on that day, inflation would last one day and then be over. The money supply and the price level would stay at their new level with no reasons for prices to change further; we would be at a new equilibrium.

Of course, in reality prices change rather slowly after an increase in the money supply, even if the money supply change is sudden and is not repeated. The economist says that prices respond with a delay or *lag*. If the response of a very sudden 10 percent increase in the money supply was spread evenly over two years, we would have five percent inflation each year. While this is inflation, it is not what we have in mind when we think of the sort of inflation the United States has known. This is not caused by once and for all jumps in the money supply, but by continuous increases in the money supply.

We should note carefully that it is only if the money supply is steadily being increased faster than the money demand that there is reason for an ongoing inflation. It follows that to turn the supply and demand for money story into a full-fledged theory of inflation we need a theory of money demand *over time*. This is a dynamic theory of money demand that must be combined with the behavior of the money supply over time. Because the supply is at the discretion of the central bank, it is difficult to predict. However, if for some reason the central bank continues to allow the money supply to grow faster than the demand we will have inflation.

While we are more used to thinking in terms of increases in the money supply, we should not neglect the effect of decreases. Indeed, these will show us the power of money. If the money supply declined after initially being equal to the money demand, the public would find itself with fewer dollars than they would like to hold. But how can they get extra money when the supply is controlled only by the central bank? The answer is they cannot. However, while the public in aggregate cannot add to the money supply, each individual can try to add to his or her own holdings. They have two ways to attempt this, and these are to sell bonds, and to hold on to more of the money they receive from their incomes.

The extent to which the public tries to add to its money holdings by selling bonds lowers bond prices. For a given coupon level this means higher interest rates. However, this is assumed to be relatively unimportant for the demand for money. Instead of studying this, Monetarists turn to the effect of the public attempting to restore their money holdings by keeping more of the money they receive as incomes.

As the public holds on to more of their incomes to replenish their bank accounts, the reduced level of purchases of goods and services tends to push down prices. If prices fall by 10 percent after a 10 percent decline in the supply of money, the public will again be happy with the money held; the national income would have fallen in proportion to the money supply, and therefore so would the money demand.

The assumption that all of the effects of changes in the money supply show up in prices, and not in real GNP and output, may have seemed reasonable when we discussed increasing the money supply if the economy was at capacity. It is not so obvious that output would be constant if the money supply were reduced. The fall in the amount spent could result in people being put out of work. Indeed, if we had not assumed the economy to be at capacity when we considered an *increase* in the money supply, some of the induced extra spending could have shown up in higher output rather than higher prices. Money, which is just pieces of paper or entries in accounts at banks, could move the economy and cause people to be put out of work or back to work.

Some readers who have already heard that the Monetarists' theory of inflation is that prices go up in proportion to the money supply may well be wondering why it took us so long to reach this conclusion. Those who wonder the most are probably those who have heard the Monetarists' theory via a direct statement of the Quantity Theory of Money, which does not take too long to describe.

While it is true that we can state the Monetarists' theory in a much shorter and more direct fashion than we already have, brevity hides many of the assumptions we made explicit. Let us present the shorter version of the Monetarists' theory by returning to an example used in the description of the real national product.

You may recall that we defined real GNP in chapter 11 by taking an example of an economy originally producing 5,000 tons of Flexiput in a year. This was selling at $1 per ton. The national income and expenditures were therefore both $5,000 per year. As our example involved no money, let us add the assumption that there are 1,000 pieces of green paper in the economy, each stating it is legal tender and worth $1. As $5,000 of goods change hands during the year, we can also say that $5,000 of money also changes hands; it just flows in the reverse direction to the goods. Furthermore, if the stock of money is $1,000, but $5,000 of money changes hands, the green paper dollars must be used an average of five times during the year.

The average number of times the dollar bills change hands to facilitate the exchange of $5,000 worth of Flexiput is known as the *velocity of circulation of money*. In our example, this is $5,000 ÷ $1,000 = 5. Because the $5,000 used in this calculation is the national income, we refer to this particular velocity as the *income velocity*. When there are transactions in the economy that are not included in the measurement of the GNP, like the buying and selling of bonds, or the payment for inputs for producing Flexiput, the *transactions velocity* differs from the income velocity. For example, while there are $5,000 of payments for finished Flexiput, there might have been $10,000 of transactions in total. If the same 1,000 pieces of green paper were used for all the transactions the income velocity is 5, but the transactions velocity is 10. Economists generally think in terms of income velocity because transactions are not recorded in official statistics. We will follow this tradition.

The explanation of inflation by using the Quantity Theory of Money starts out by assuming that the income velocity is constant. This assumption is frequently rationalized as follows:

Most of the money stock is bank balances at commercial banks. The work that is done by the $1,000 of money in our example is therefore primarily in the form of the transfer of balances from person to person in paying for the production and consumption of the $5,000 of Flexiput. Consequently, the speed or velocity of circulation is determined by the technology or efficiency of the banking system. It is said that the technology of banking does not change from day to day, and in the short run it can be assumed to be constant. Therefore, the $1,000 of money is not likely on average to be used more or less than five times a year, so we can therefore treat the velocity of circulation as constant.

This is all we need for a theory of inflation. If the velocity of money is fixed at, for example, 5, and then the money supply is increased by 10 percent, that is, from $1,000 to $1,100, we have 5 × $1,100 = $5,500 being paid for Flexiput after the money supply increase. If the output of Flexiput is still 5,000 tons and $5,500 is being paid for these, the average price must be $1.10 per ton. This is a 10 percent price increase brought about by a 10 percent increase in the money supply. The Monetarists' conclusion: Prices rise in proportion to the money supply.

The fact that we derive the same conclusion from directly applying the Quantity Theory as from our previous description of supply for money versus the demand for money does not mean we have avoided the need to make assumptions. In particular, we are still assuming that the demand for money is proportionate to income and does not depend greatly on the interest rate. These assumptions are hidden in the assumptions of constant velocity of circulation of money. It would be odd, indeed, if by thinking differently within the same context we could have saved on assumptions; there are no free lunches with economic theories, as well as with what the theories explain. Because economists spend a considerable amount of time reconciling different theories, it will do us no harm to reflect on why the constant velocity assumption boils down to the assumptions made in the previous explanation of Monetarists' thinking.

We recall that the income velocity of circulation of money is merely the national income divided by the quantity of money that supports this income. In our example, it is $5,000 ÷ $1,000 before the money supply was increased, and $5,500 ÷ $1,100 afterward; in either case the velocity is 5. We can see from the calculation of velocity in our example that as the national income goes up, the amount of money that people hold—which is assumed to be what they want to hold—goes up in the same proportion. We should recall that this is the very assumption we made when presenting the Monetarists' view of the demand for money earlier. The constant velocity assumption hence means the same as the proportionality assumption, that is, the demand for money is proportional to expenditures. We can also notice that in assuming a constant velocity we are assuming that if there is any reduction of interest rates caused by an increase in the money supply, this does not then increase money demand. Otherwise, the amount of money held relative to income would be increasing as the money supply is increased due to the lower opportunity cost. It follows, therefore, that the assumptions that the demand for money changes in proportion to national income, and that the demand is invariant to interest rates, will produce the constant velocity assumed in the direct presentation of the Quantity Theory.

It may help some to think of the Monetarists' theory of inflation as saying that whatever the supply of money happens to be, it always buys the same quantity of goods. The quantity of goods is the real GNP, which is the available supply. It is difficult to buy more than this, certainly as long as we don't include international trade. In our example, money can buy the available supply, which is 5,000 tons of Flexiput. This is true whether the money supply is $1,000 or $1,100. All that happens when the money supply is increased by 10 percent is that the value of each dollar declines by 10 percent, and each Flexiput unit requires 10 percent more dollars.

As we said at the beginning of this chapter the thinking of the Monetarist fits into the general theory of supply and demand. As in the general theory of supply and demand, when the supply goes up the price or value declines. In the case of money, as the supply goes up its value declines, that is, it won't buy as much because prices are higher. However, we also have a quantitative prediction in the case of money, namely that the value of each unit of money declines at the same percentage rate as the supply is increased. This follows as long as the real output is fixed. But what if output is not fixed?

As we have already mentioned, Monetarists believe that the amount of money we wish to hold for convenience depends on the dollar amount we spend. It does not matter whether this changes because of prices or because of changes in real expenditures. The amount we leave home with in the morning is determined by the amount we expect to have to pay for newspapers, meals, and so on. Having to take more bus rides or paying more for each ride both have the same effect on the demand for money. More generally, money demand is related to nominal GNP, not real GNP.

Because of the irrelevance of the composition of changes in nominal GNP between prices and real output, the Monetarist believes that every increase in the real GNP reduces inflation by the same percentage. For example, if the money supply goes up by 10 percent during a period when real GNP goes up by the same amount, there is no need for the increased supply of money to cause inflation. The 10 percent higher real income and expenditures will cause the demand for money to increase by 10 percent, which will match the increase in the money supply, reestablishing equilibrium. There will therefore be no attempt to take the extra money and buy bonds or goods. The increased money supply will be demanded and held.

In general, the inflation that results from increasing the

money supply will be the difference between the rate at which the supply of money is increasing, and the rate at which real GNP is increasing. Therefore, it is only by increasing the supply of money faster than the real GNP is growing that there is more money per goods available and hence inflation.

You may recall that at the end of the previous chapter we said that, at least during recessions, the Keynesians believe that increasing the money supply will have no effect on peoples' spending as they will merely hold on to the money. You might be thinking that this probably occurs because at the time of a severe recession the extra money will increase the real output, and that it is this that makes people want to hold onto their money. But in fact, the Keynesians have a very different notion in mind, which relates to the interest rate. At this point we should review the assumptions concerning interest rates used by the Keynesians and the Monetarists, for these are at the center of the differences in thinking.

Keynesians agree with the Monetarists that people must choose whether to hold their wealth in the form of bonds or money. They also agree that money offers more convenience in the form of certain buying power and the absence of brokerage costs, but involves an opportunity cost. However, the Keynesians believe that as interest rates decline, people may eventually believe they are unlikely to decline further. Indeed, when rates are very low they may seem more likely to increase than decrease. This makes the holding of bonds extremely risky, and it also means a very low opportunity cost of holding money. After all, if interest rates do increase, the market value of bonds—which is the present value of bond coupons—is reduced, and those who hold bonds would have been better off to have held money instead.

As a result of their way of thinking, the Keynesians assume that as interest rates go down, eventually there is a large demand for money. This is called a *speculative demand* and this motive for holding money becomes more powerful at lower interest rates. When interest rates are extremely low, as they were during the Great Depression, the opportunity cost of holding money becomes so low, and the risk so high, that there is an unlimited speculative demand for money— a *Liquidity Trap*. This is why the Keynesians say that at low interest rates the demand for money increases considerably as a result of further declines in interest rates. The Monetarists counter that while the Keynesian view may well be correct during severe recessions, these are infrequent, and in more normal times about as many people think interest rates will go up as down, resulting in no sure bets.

An alternative way of thinking of the differences between the Keynesians and Monetarists is that Keynesians believe the velocity of circulation of money could change according to any number of factors, especially according to interest rates, while Monetarists think it is constant, or at least predictable. In particular, Keynesians believe that when the money supply is increased the velocity could decline leaving no change in the nominal GNP. For example, when the money supply goes up by 10 percent from $1,000 to $1,100 as in our last example, if the velocity fell 10 percent from 5 to 4.5, the total of dollars spent would be $4,950 (4.5 × $1,100). This is approximately the same as the nominal GNP before the money supply was increased. If velocity is as volatile as this, money has little or no effect on national output, however it is measured.

A low interest rate is not the only factor a Keynesian thinks will make velocity variable. Many Keynesians think velocity is so unstable that it can jump around almost without explanation. A story which they might like to use to illustrate the instability of velocity was provided by the British economist F. Y. Edgeworth, long before the time of Keynes. The story tells of two enterprising men, Bob and Joe, who decided to pull a cart containing a barrel of beer to the fair on Derby Day. The beer was to sell at sixpence a glass.

The day was hot, and the cart was heavy, and it was not long before Joe developed a fiery thirst. He felt in his pocket and found a threepence.

"Bob," he said, "Would you mind if I took a glass of beer and gave you this threepence, which is your share of what we would receive for the glass at the fair?"

"Of course!" said Bob, as this is indeed what he would get.

The two labored on their way and before long it was Bob who had a severe thirst. He felt the threepence in his pocket that he had received from Joe and asked if he could buy a beer for Joe's half share.

"Of course!" was the reply, and they went on their progressively merrier way until the obvious happened.

The threepence that traveled between this amiable pair did a remarkable amount of work. We might presume that its velocity, which can be thought of as the value of beer divided by threepence, would not have been so large had the day been cooler. We have an example where the money in circulation could have achieved whatever transactions occurred. But is this the case in normal circumstances when money is moving on the ledgers of banks and not from pocket to pocket between good friends?

Whether velocity is indeed stable over time or whether it can be whatever is required to clear the market is an entirely empirical matter. In order to make the determination it is necessary to study velocity from year to year to see if it behaves smoothly or whether it is volatile. Alternatively, we must see whether the demand for money does consistently move up and down in proportion to nominal expenditures, or at least in a predictable way. Unfortunately, the research papers on this question could fill dozens of books of this size. It is testimony to the fact that the question remains unsettled that there are still economists rigidly adhering to either the Monetarist or the Keynesian camp.

CHAPTER 14

Thinking Sensibly

Reconciling Different Views on Inflation

> When I see something that makes absolutely no sense whatever, I figure there must be a damn good reason for it. PETER DE VRIES

> ... Money, which is a source of so many blessings to mankind, becomes also, unless we can control it, a source of peril and confusion.
> SIR DENIS H. ROBERTSON

HAVING PRESENTED the two major schools of thought on inflation, we should see how they compare to the opinions of non-economists. Recall that we had listed a number of frequently heard opinions—that inflation is due to excessive wage demands by trade unions, unwarranted price increases by greedy businessmen, the power of outside commodity cartels like OPEC, and the deficit spending of governments. Only the final item has been met in our explanation of economic thinking, and then only in connection with the Keynesians. However, it turns out that all these commonly held opinions can fit into the thinking of both schools of macroeconomics.

THINKING BIG

Careful thinking reveals that the opinions of many non-economists refer to high prices rather than inflation. This is true even of such popular notions that inflation is caused by trade unions or monopolistic practices.

When we restrict supply we raise prices. This is true both of labor, where we raise wages, and of the products people buy. However, a high price is not the same as inflation. As we have already said, inflation refers to increasing prices, so while a union may get its members 50 percent more than they would otherwise have earned, provided union wages remain 50 percent higher and all other wages are constant, the union does not contribute toward inflation. This is an important part of thinking of all economists, Monetarist and Keynesian, so we should clarify the point.

If prices and nonunion wages are steady, the only way a union can achieve continuing increases in the wages of its members is by greater and greater restrictions on labor supply which would create a union without members. Affecting the level of wages is different from affecting the rate at which wages are changing. Unions cannot force wages up for very long, and even if they could it would not mean inflation, which by definition refers to prices, not wages. High wages are quite distinct from increasing wages and even more distinct from increasing prices.

While unions cannot directly affect inflation even if they can achieve higher wage rates, according to the thinking of both major schools of macroeconomic thought they can indirectly be responsible for inflation by either causing an increasing fiscal deficit or a steadily increasing money supply.

As we have already learned, when the price of any

product or service is increased, quantity demanded declines and quantity supplied goes up. Therefore, higher wages due to union restrictions means more people wanting to work at the union wages, as well as a lower demand for workers by employers. By definition, this is unemployment that is calculated as the fraction of the workforce willing to work but who cannot find jobs. Eventually the unemployment should begin to decline as those unable to find jobs in the unionized sector find jobs elsewhere. However, the government may be sympathetic to the anguish and suffering of the unemployed while they are looking for jobs. The government may therefore try to create more jobs by stimulating the economy, either by running fiscal deficits causing net injections into the flow of income or by printing more money. If this pattern continues, with wage increases followed by expansionary macroeconomic policy, inflation will result. It is in this indirect way that unions can be a factor behind inflation, so the everyday argument is consistent with both schools of thought. However, while the opinion of the non-economist may well be correct it requires a lot more careful thinking than the argument suggests.

Let us turn to another group frequently blamed for inflation, that of the businessmen with monopoly power. According to the thinking of economists, can monopolistic businessmen cause inflation by continually raising prices?

As in the case of unions we must take great care to distinguish high prices from increasing prices. Only the latter is inflation. Even if businessmen can achieve high prices for their products by using monopoly power to restrict supply, it is completely different from making prices go higher and higher, that is, causing inflation.

Increasing prices require more and more supply restrictions. In other words, businessmen can cause inflation only if they can exercise more and more stringent supply restrictions. However, with ever decreasing supply they would be receiving higher prices on ever declining sales, which would eventually reduce their profits if demand were elastic. (Recall that elastic demand means sales fall by a greater percentage than prices increase, and that all firms with control over prices produce where their demand is elastic. It is for this reason that maximizing profits does not result from maximizing prices.)

Monopolistic practices by businessmen, as with monopolistic practices by unions, can achieve high prices (or wages) but they cannot sustain increases without some help by the government. However, as with wage increases initiated by the unions, governments may well respond to high prices by increasing the supply of money or by running fiscal deficits. But why should they want to do this? It is here that the Monetarist's thinking comes to the forefront. This is because while a higher level of prices has no obvious implications for the circular flow of income, other than that it would become generally larger, it has a very powerful implication for the demand for money.

A higher price level, as we have learned from our explanation of the Monetarists' view of the demand for money, will also cause an increase in the amount of money the public wants to hold. Indeed, according to the Monetarists, the public's demand for money should increase in the same proportion as the price level.

Can the public get the extra money it demands? Because the money supply is not controlled by the public, it cannot raise the supply, but as individuals, the public can try to get more money by selling bonds and by spending a smaller fraction of incomes. The selling of bonds will lower bond prices, thereby raising interest rates, and the reduction in the fraction of income spent will mean declining product demand. While the interest rate increase will have little effect on money demand according to Monetarists' thinking, the fall in demand for products will tend to undo the problem we began with, that is, an increased price level. However, the drop in demand for goods might cause workers to be fired while, or even before, prices decline. After all, it can take quite a drop in demand to cause *deflation,* or declining prices. This is where the government may step in.

As in the case of unemployment caused by too high wages, rather than accept the toll of rising unemployment, governments may decide that a stimulation in demand is required. This stimulation can take the form of an increase in the fiscal deficit or in the supply of money, either of which could be inflationary depending on your chosen economic school. As we have already mentioned in chapter 12, because of the way the situation occurs it is called *accommodation.* When the problem starts with wages we might refer to it as *wage accommodation,* and when it is due to the power of businessmen we might call it *price accommodation.* However, it should be clear that while both schools of thought can explain inflation via wage accommodation it is only the Monetarists that can explain why price accommodation will occur because it comes via an increase in the demand for money.

Inflation from increases in oil prices that has been attributed to OPEC is, of course, related to the inflation caused by businessmen we have just described. However, in this special case the accommodation can be more direct and explained by both the Keynesians and the Monetarists.

When it is only oil prices that increase, more of consumers' incomes must be channeled into heating their homes and fueling their cars, reducing income available for other products. Unemployment is likely when this fall in demand occurs, especially if extra jobs do not simultaneously appear in the energy sector, as happens when the oil is imported. If the government does not act the prices of products other than oil would eventually fall due to declining demand. This would reduce the cost for those items, offsetting the higher oil prices. Indeed, in the end the overall cost of living could be unchanged, with more expensive energy and cheaper food, cars, and so forth. However, the government may act before non-oil prices have declined and stimulate demand in the non-oil industries. This may take the form of an expanding money supply or of increased fiscal deficits, and in this way the oil price increase can be inflationary.

Up to this point, we have described how both schools of thought can explain inflation started by supply restrictions, whether of labor or goods, but we have not explained how a Monetarist views fiscal deficits. Can a Monetarist see fiscal deficits as inflationary?

The strict Monetarist reasons that if the government spends in excess of what it collects in taxes, it can finance the consequent deficit in one of two ways. It can borrow from the public or it can monetize its debt, that is, print more money.

If the government uses borrowing from the public to finance its deficit, and if the deficit does cause product prices to increase, the Monetarist reasons that this will increase money demand. This is because with higher prices the public wants to hold more money for regular expenditures. But where is the public going to get the extra money they demand? If the deficit is financed by borrowing, there is no change in the supply of money to match the extra demand. However, each individual can try to get more money away from others by selling bonds or reducing spending. Collectively this cannot work, but these actions will put upward pressure on interest rates (via lowering bond prices as they are sold) and downward pressure on prices (via the reduction in spending). If the higher interest rates do not dampen the demand for money by raising the opportunity cost, the downward pressure on prices will end only when the money demand is where it was before the government deficit occurred. This requires that prices and expenditures end up back where they started before the deficit was incurred.

What we have just said is not straightforward and it will serve us well to review it carefully. We have said that according to the thinking of Monetarists, if a deficit financed by the government selling bills and bonds did raise prices, it would thereby raise money demand. This in turn would cause bond prices to decline (and hence interest rates to increase) and cause a fall in consumer demand. These changes would stop only when prices are at their initial level. Therefore, it follows that deficits cannot cause inflation—not, at least, to strict Monetarists.

The type of thinking we have just used is of a special variety. We have shown that if an event—like a fiscal deficit—did have a particular effect—like increasing the price level—this could not represent a new equilibrium. This type of thinking was also used when we spoke of the Monetarists' thinking about what would happen if monopolies raised prices. In both cases, we have rejected assumed outcomes by showing that if the assumed outcomes did occur they would have implications which would eventually undo the assumed outcomes. In effect, this method of thinking involves exploring logical consistency. But could a government deficit ever be inflationary, or is it always ruled out by a logical inconsistency?

If the government deficit is financed by printing money rather than selling bonds, and if we assume, as we did before, that the deficit causes an increase in prices, the higher prices could be sustained. This is because as prices and consequently money demand go up, these can be matched by the increasing money supply the government is using to finance its deficit. There is then no need for the public to sell bonds and reduce spending to obtain more money—which cannot succeed in the aggregate anyway. Therefore, we reach the Monetarists' conclusion that prices rise in proportion to the money supply, but to a Monetarist it is the printing of money used to finance the deficit that causes higher prices, not the deficit itself.

Economic thinking can be applied to check the validity of a view held by many non-economists that the extreme form of inflation, *hyperinflation* or "galloping inflation," can be caused by an initially limited amount of inflation feeding on itself. The non-economists have in mind a scenario in which, because prices are rising, consumers are tempted to buy immediately rather than wait until prices are higher. This makes prices rise even more, causing more consumers to rush into purchasing, and so on, ad nauseum. The stampede to buy in order to save on paying more later causes prices to rise at tremendous rates. But can this sort of panic buying scenario occur?

On the question of hyperinflation, Monetarists and many Keynesians concur that speculative fires are unable to burn for very long without being fueled by a rapidly increasing money supply. Otherwise, higher prices would raise the demand for money relative to the fixed supply causing reduced spending as the public attempted to obtain the extra cash balances. Put differently, if the supply of money were constant, to support the higher prices the velocity of circulation of money would have to be unbelievably high. However, there are limits on the speed with which money circulates, so that galloping inflation, with prices rising by thousands or millions of percent per annum, must be caused by a galloping money supply. The thinking of the non-economist may be correct for short periods of time, but cannot explain the crazy hyperinflations that have occurred in Europe and South America.

While Monetarists generally explain inflation in terms of a continually increasing money supply, we should note that inflation can also result from a reduction in money demand. It will help us check our thinking to show how this occurs.

Assume that the microcomputer revolution enables a large number of households to fine tune their cash flows, keeping track of what is spent and earned, so that they can maintain minimal cash balances. Such a money-management revolution, which would result in a reduction in the demand for money, would mean that for a fixed supply of money the supply will exceed the demand. People would try to move out of money and into bonds and goods. But as we have learned, the money supply is affected not by the efforts of individuals, but by the central bank. As individuals try to get out of money they will raise the price of bonds, therefore reducing interest rates, and raise prices of goods. According to the Monetarists' assumptions, the reduced interest rates will not have much effect on increasing the demand for money, but the higher prices of goods will. Eventually, higher prices will reincrease the demand for money until it again equals the unchanged money supply.

The forgoing scenario was caused by a revolution in the use of microcomputers. It could also result from the expanded use of credit cards. These allow us to economize on the amount of money we hold because settlement dates are predictable. Indeed, if all payments were on cards we would need money in our checking account only on the date of settlement. In this way, credit cards are inflationary. However, this is because of the effect on money demand, not because of the effect of credit cards on the money supply.

While we can use economic thinking to reach the same conclusions as non-economists and to develop further conclusions, there are limitations to the economic way of thinking. Most particular, there are serious limits in the economists' ability to predict inflation because of their inability to predict the factors behind it.

What the Keynesian needs in order to turn the circular flow of income into a method of prediction is some means of predicting the relevant injections and withdrawals. But how can we predict business investment, exports, and government spending? Even Keynes believed that business investment was determined by "animal spirits," and about all we know of government spending is that it generally grows. We are unlikely to do much better predicting withdrawals like savings, taxes, and imports. Hence, even if the circular flow of income is an excellent way of describing the factors behind inflation, it does not help us in making forecasts.

The Monetarists' way of thinking about inflation is no

better at making predictions as it also requires predicting the exogenous factors. Even if it were true that inflation rates were precisely determined by growth in the money supply as it is when velocity of circulation is constant, we cannot use this to predict inflation in the future. For this we need to determine future money supply growth. This is a question that goes beyond economics as it is practiced. However, because money supply growth depends on the beliefs of politicians and central bankers there is no reason why we could not make the behavior of money supply endogenous.

To some extent, a statistical analysis of historical data can be used to see what bankers have responded to in the past. For example, it may be determined that the money supply has been expanded more when unemployment has been high or when spending has been slack. Another factor that may help is knowing where—in which university—the central bankers studied economics. This is a factor considered by some professional experts trying to predict the path of exchange rates, which also depend on the decisions of central bankers.

Even if we could predict the changes in the money supply or in injections and withdrawals we would still have difficulties predicting monthly or even annual rates of inflation. This is because inflation responds to the respective stimuli with a lag. The lags are an empirical matter and the evidence indicates that macroeconomic changes have long and variable lagged effects on inflation. Consequently, even if we could predict that the money supply would grow at 10 percent during the coming year, we would not know when the 10 percent increase in prices would take place. Moreover, we would also need to predict the money demand.

Another major limitation to the power of thinking like an economist is that we do not know which economists think well. This is as true when we are concerned with unemployment, as it is with inflation.

CHAPTER 15

Thinking Rationally

The Causes of Unemployment

> The definition of a living wage depends on whether
> you are getting it or giving it.   EVAN ESAR

> You can't make up for lost time by the unemployed.
>   Anonymous

THE THINKING of Keynesians and Monetarists on the
question of unemployment is at least as different as it is
for inflation. And just as in the case of inflation, it requires
a stretching of the mind to adapt the ideas of either school
of thought in order to reach the conclusions popular with
non-economists.

As we have already mentioned, Keynesians view unemployment in much the same way as they view inflation,
again employing the framework of the circular flow of
income. They believe that the cause of unemployment is
withdrawals from the circular flow exceeding new injections.
This can be either because desired savings exceed desired
investment, because imports exceed exports, or because
taxes exceed government spending. (Few people worry

about taxes exceeding government spending. Fiscal surpluses are not exactly common.)

To summarize what we said in chapter 12, desired savings can exceed investment when interest rates cannot drop sufficiently to make them equal. This requires that interest rates are already low, or that both savings and investment are insensitive to changes in interest rates. If a drop in interest rates cannot make savings equal to desired investment the net withdrawals this implies will lower income. This generally concurs with an increase in unemployment.

Keynesians have other explanations of unemployment that are based on other reasons why the equality of injections and withdrawals is not obtained. We have already mentioned the persistent inequality of government spending and taxes, which are primarily politically determined and therefore rarely equal, and in the case of exports and imports an imbalance can be attributed to problems with exchange rates.

We have pointed out that Keynesians realize that even if withdrawals do exceed injections this does not cause unemployment if wages fall. Then the lower circular flow of income caused by net withdrawals just means every person will have a lower income but all will be working. Real output is unchanged—the same amount of work means the same real GNP. Therefore, the standard of living is also unchanged. After all, the standard of living we enjoy is determined by the number of loaves of bread and new cars produced, not by the number of dollars and cents in our paychecks. However, as Keynes realized, wages do not drop readily, so unemployment and reduced living standards result when withdrawals exceed injections.

Monetarists also blame incorrect wages for unemployment. However, they do not explain why wages are incorrect in terms of the circular flow of income. Rather, they use the fact that wages are contracted in advance according to anticipated future inflation. It is when the actually experienced rate of inflation differs from what had been expected that the contracted wages are incorrect. This reasoning is not straightforward and requires careful explanation.

When contracted wages are increasing at the same rate as eventually realized inflation, there is no reason for employers to hire more or less workers. This is because the prices of what they are selling, which are going up at the inflation rate, are covering their increasing wage bill. However, if for some reason wages are increasing at a faster rate than inflation, employers will find costs rising faster than product prices. Profit margins would be squeezed and they would cut back on production and employment. Alternatively, if wages are increasing more slowly than the prices of what employers are selling, we can expect the larger margins of output prices over costs to encourage employers to add to their workforce.

Monetarists realize that the situation of wages increasing faster than inflation is likely to occur when inflation anticipated by workers exceeds the eventually realized inflation. This is because wages are negotiated for future contract periods according to the rate at which the cost of living is expected to increase. When the actually realized inflation is below previous expectations, contracted wages are too high and unemployment increases. But when is this situation likely to occur?

The rate of inflation that workers expect during their

contract period is most likely based on recent inflationary experience. For example, if inflation has been steady at 5 percent, workers are likely to anticipate that it will continue at 5 percent. If this is so, it follows that inflation will be overestimated most often when it is declining. Therefore, Monetarists believe that unemployment will increase at times when inflation is falling. This they in turn link to reductions in the rate of increase in the money supply. So Monetarists believe that unemployment is likely to increase when the monetary authorities decide to reduce the growth rate of money.

The other side to the Monetarists' thinking is that unemployment will fall when inflation is underestimated by workers. In this case, wages will undercompensate for the realized increases in the prices of what employers sell. With larger profit margins while wage contracts are valid, employers are likely to expand. Such a situation may occur when inflation is increasing. As Monetarists think this happens when the rate of increase of the money supply is also increasing, they believe that declines in unemployment are caused by more rapid expansion in the money supply.

It is important to keep in mind that it is the inflexibility of wages relative to the prices of what employers are selling that drives the Monetarists' theory. For example, it is only if wage rates do not fall in line with falling inflation, when inflation has been overestimated, that unemployment is likely to accompany declining inflation.

Monetarists do not believe that inflation will be overestimated or underestimated for long. Hence, their belief that unemployment increases with declining inflation, and decreases with increasing inflation, constitutes only a short-run theory of unemployment. In the long run, Monetarists argue that workers will see what has happened and readjust future wage contracts accordingly. Hence, if they did overestimate inflation and therefore negotiated wages that were too high causing increased unemployment, future wage contracts would reflect the lower realized inflation. Then, the unemployment rate would drop as wages became appropriate again.

The rate of unemployment that emerges in the long run is often referred to as the *natural rate of unemployment*. In the short run, a decrease in inflation and consequent above equilibrium wages could get unemployment above this rate, but eventually the natural rate would be restored. Similarly, increasing inflation and consequent below equilibrium wages may well get unemployment below the natural rate, but not indefinitely. Any benefit of reduced unemployment from increasing inflation is therefore short run, and if the higher rate of inflation is maintained and eventually estimated correctly, unemployment will return to normal. There are no free lunches from increasing inflation because it cannot permanently reduce unemployment.

Many economists refer to the relation between inflation and unemployment as the Phillips Curve, after the economist who studied the evidence for Great Britain. The Phillips Curve is usually described as showing that if we are prepared to tolerate higher inflation we can have lower unemployment. What we have said is that it is increasing inflation, not high inflation, that lowers unemployment. We have also said that even increasing inflation cannot lower unemployment in the long run. This is because workers will learn what has happened, raise wages, and eliminate the reason for employers to increase hirings.

According to the thinking of Monetarists, the natural rate of unemployment is not necessarily constant. It is influenced by such factors as the benefits received by workers when they are unemployed, the rate at which the structure of industry is changing, and so forth. However these changes are gradual.

Since the 1970s, some economists have emerged from the Monetarists' camp who take the argument further. These economists are known as the Rational Expectationists, and according to their way of thinking inflation cannot lower unemployment, even in the short run.

The Rational Expectationists believe that workers think rationally, taking into account more than just past inflation when forming their expectations about the future. For example, they look at such factors as money supply growth, fiscal deficits, and so on, and even if they are unable to weigh the evidence, they hire professional personnel who can. Therefore, increasing inflation is not sufficient to cause declining unemployment, because the increase will on average be correctly anticipated: Future inflation should be evident in the economic factors behind the inflation, and everyone can observe these factors.

Rational Expectationists believe that the government cannot fool workers by using expansionary policy to get unemployment to decline. However, they do not believe that unemployment will therefore always equal the natural rate, but rather that unemployment randomly hovers around this level. Errors in forecasting are made by workers, but these are not systematic and are not controllable by the monetary authorities. Consequently, monetary and fiscal policy are inept vis-à-vis the unemployment rate, and the government should give up on discretionary macroeconomic policy.

Many of the Rational Expectationists are Monetarists who believe in the Quantity Theory. However, they believe money can affect only inflation as in the Quantity Theory, and can have no "real" effects on employment or real GNP other than a detrimental one, by adding to uncertainty.

If we return to the opinions on unemployment held by many non-economists we can see how they fit into the thinking of the different schools of macroeconomists. We recall that among the most commonly heard opinions among non-economists is that unemployment is caused by labor-saving machinery and technology.

Labor-saving machines may lower the wages at which employers would use people rather than machines. If before self-serve pumps became available at gas stations it would have been worth paying $5 per hour for an attendant; it may be worth only $2 per hour when the alternative machines are available.

If we think of machines as lowering the wage rates at which people would be employed, we see that both Keynesians and Monetarists could entertain the idea of unemployment caused by new technology; it makes current wages inappropriate. However, the effect of machines can be even more directly integrated into both schools of thought.

Monetarists believe that the natural rate of unemployment is affected by such factors as the rate at which new technology is introduced, and the rate at which shifts in demand for different products occur. Changes in technology and demand are referred to as *structural changes*. If, for example, there are increasingly rapid shifts in demand like those from slide rules to electronic calculators, or from spring-driven to quartz watches, there will be an increase in the natural unemployment rate—the displaced take time to locate new opportunities and must then be trained. Keynesians also incorporate structural unemployment in their theory by adding this to the unemployment caused by reductions in the circular flow of income. We find that while neither of the schools has the unemployment that results from labor-saving machinery as an essential facet of their theory, they can both accommodate it.

Competition from abroad is a direct part of the Keynesian way of thinking about unemployment, but is only indirectly related to Monetarist thinking. As we have mentioned, imports represent a withdrawal from a country's circular flow of income while exports are an injection. If because of cheap overseas products imports are increasing relative to exports, there will be net withdrawals, a decline in the flow of income, and with rigid wages, an increase in unemployment. Monetarists do not have a straightforward answer. However, they might say that the availability of goods from abroad may make previously negotiated wages too high, causing temporary unemployment in the same way that it is caused by overestimation of inflation.

There is little disagreement between Keynesians and Monetarists on the potential role of trade unions in keeping wages above the level for full employment. However, the two major schools of thought differ completely on what types of government policies they consider cause wages to exceed the "correct" level.

Keynesians believe that wages can be too high if the government spends too little. Because government spending is an injection into the circular flow of income, reduced spending can cause unemployment when wages are not revised downward. Monetarists prefer to explain too high wages in terms of overestimation of inflation due to a reduction in the growth rate of the money supply. However, those Monetarists who believe in rational expectations would not agree to this. Indeed, Rational Expectationists might even reach the opposite conclusion to the Keynesians, arguing that increasing deficits from higher government spending could indirectly cause more unemployment. This could happen via the higher real interest rates brought about by government borrowing to cover deficits that crowd out private borrowing. This, plus the fear of future inflation if the debt-financed deficits are eventually monetized, could raise interest rates so much that it could cause unemployment in the private sector. We find that a case can be made for too little or too much government spending causing unemployment, opinions frequently heard from non-economists.

The popular view that unemployment can be caused by an influx into the workforce of groups like immigrants or working wives can fit into economic thinking, but only by bringing in wage inflexibility. This is because if wages are free to vary full employment is ensured because the supply and demand for labor would then be equal, whatever the supply. This conclusion is related to what is called Say's Law, after French economist Jean Baptiste Say, who argued that if people spend their income, or somebody spends what people save as savings are recycled by banks, the circular flow of income must remain steady. However, if additions to the workforce lower the wage at which the labor market is in equilibrium, but the actual wage does not decline, wages are too high and unemployment could result. But why does the market clearing wage decline when the addition to the workforce will add to output as well as demand? The Monetarists have the answer.

For a given supply of money, an increased output due to extra workers would lower the price level. The lower cost of living would mean that nominal wages could fall and still leave people just as well off as they were. However, institutional rigidities like unions and contracts prevent wages from falling, meaning that wages are too high for full employment. Consequently, while there is no necessity for additional workers to cause additional unemployment it is likely to occur. As Keynesians look at injections and withdrawals, they might not reach this conclusion.

Both Keynesian and Monetarist thinking can provide explanations of unemployment not frequently heard from non-economists. A Keynesian might argue unemployment is sometimes the result of people increasing savings or the result of government increasing taxes to eliminate fiscal deficits. A Monetarist could argue that unemployment is the result of an increased demand for money, which has the same effect as a reduction in the money supply—that is, reduced spending. They can also argue that unemployment can be reduced by increasing the frequency of renegotiating wage contracts, since this should make wages inappropriate for a shorter period. There are many more rich implications in thinking economically about unemployment, like the effects of minimum wage laws and unemployment benefits which probably occurred to you as you read this chapter.

CHAPTER 16

Thinking Effectively

The Effects of Money and Inflation

> He is no mean philosopher who can give a reason for one half of what he thinks.   WILLIAM HAZLITT

> The national debt proves that America is less a government of checks and balances and more a government of checks than balances.   EVAN ESAR

IT IS on the effects of inflation and unemployment rather than on their causes that economic thinking provides its more important insights. This is particularly true for the economist's thinking about effects of inflation.

Many people without economic training think inflation makes them poorer. They have in mind the negative impact of a higher cost of living on the buying power of their incomes. "If only the cost of living were not increasing, my income increase would really be worth something!" Somehow or other they believe lower inflation would leave their gains in income intact. Furthermore, they believe that inflation is particularly damaging to those like the retired who are living out of savings because they must live on a fixed income.

THINKING BIG

Economists know that our standard of living is determined by real GNP. Inflation can affect nominal GNP, but the real GNP is determined by the resources that are employed—labor, capital, and raw materials—and the technology with which they are combined. Inflation is not part of the real GNP, and provided nominal incomes increase at the same rate as prices, the real GNP is not affected. Indeed, increasing prices could occur with all of us becoming better off provided our nominal incomes are growing at a faster rate than prices. The evidence shows that in the long run this is certainly the case, as our standard of living has improved over the years despite a rising cost of living.

While economists do not think of inflation making us poorer, they do know an indirect route by which inflation could have a small effect on our living standards. This is an effect which is unlikely to show up in any regularly published economic statistics but is worth mentioning.

Inflation makes it more costly to hold money, like currency and checking accounts, which do not bear interest. This is because inflation makes the buying power of our dollar bills and funds in our zero-interest checking accounts decline. Therefore, as inflation increases we reduce the amount of the wealth we hold in the form of money. However, money provides us with convenience, which we can think of as a service. Indeed, we have already pointed out how large a service this is; each dollar held without interest when it could have been invested at 10 percent, costs us 10 cents per year to hold, and therefore must provide us with at least 10 cents of convenience or liquidity services. It follows that if inflation makes us economize on money we lose the services provided by the money, which is a cost to each of us. This cost does not appear in the statistics on real GNP because GNP does not include the services of money balances as a specific output item. However, we are individually and collectively worse off if we reduce our money holdings because we lose some of the convenience money provides.

Instead of thinking in terms of inflation making us worse off, the economist thinks of inflation as redistributing real income and wealth. The most obvious redistribution is from those who demand money to those that supply it.

A revealing way of demonstrating how inflation can redistribute real income and wealth is in the answer to a popular examination question. The question, which has appeared in exams at the University of Chicago and elsewhere, deals with an Englishman on vacation on an agreeable island. The Englishman was in the habit of paying for everything by check, which the islanders accepted because the Englishman was well known and undoubtedly honest. Indeed, the Englishman's honesty was so apparent that the islanders were prepared to accept the Englishman's checks from each other, and these were never returned to the Englishman's bank in London for debiting against his checking (or chequing) account. The question that is asked is, "Who paid for the Englishman's vacation?"

It should be clear that the Englishman did not pay. It should also be clear that it is not the last person holding the checks, because each person can spend them. Who then did pay? Could it be no one paid?

If the total output on the island was not affected by the Englishman being there on vacation, and if he enjoyed some of the island's output, then the islanders must have gone without something. Hence, if the output was fixed, the islanders did pay, by an amount equal to what the Englishman consumed. But how was this amount transferred from the islanders? If we apply economic thinking we see that it was transferred via inflation caused by the increase in the island's money supply.

The money supply grew because the general acceptability of the Englishman's checks made the checks into money. According to the thinking of Monetarists, the increased money supply would cause inflation, which would lower the buying power of the island's preexisting money. Therefore, those people holding preexisting money paid for the Englishman's vacation. Because at some time or another the preexisting money would have been held by almost everyone, all the islanders paid; the more money they held, the more they paid. There was a transfer of income from the islanders to the vacationing Englishman according to the islanders' holdings of the preexisting money.

This answer is preferred by economists who believe that the Englishman's vacation would not affect the output of the island. However, if his injection of spending, or of money, caused an increase in the island's output, the islanders might not have had to forgo consumption. The Englishman could have consumed goods and services made by people who otherwise would have been unemployed. Because it could be either the injection—spending by tourists is an export—or the increased money supply that increased output, it is consistent with both major schools of thought to say that nobody needed to have paid. Only the Monetarists of the Rational Expectations variety might feel that output was not affected by the extra money or by the extra injection.

If the island's output was unaffected by the Englishman's

vacation we can say that he enjoyed his consumption via an inflation "tax." Most often, the inflation tax is borne when the government adds to the supply of money. The government consumes goods and services with the money it prints. Therefore we must pay, provided the extra government spending or money does not increase output by an equal amount. We pay the tax on our cash balances, which fall in purchasing power by an equivalent amount to the purchases of the government.

Another example of the power of inflation to transfer real buying power from money holders or demanders, to money makers or suppliers, is the effect of the introduction of counterfeit bills into circulation. It should be clear that if counterfeiters enjoy some of a fixed national output, we cash holders, not those accepting the bills, are those that pay.

If we examine the transfer of wealth via deflation from money destruction rather than expansion, we see not only the transfer of buying power from money destroyers to money holders. We also see an important difference between the value of money to an individual and its value to society.

Some time ago I was told of a professor of economics who used to walk into his class when the subject was money, and set fire to a dollar bill. "Why do you look so shocked?" the professor would ask his bemused students. "I have destroyed nothing of value. It's just a piece of paper, like any other in the wastepaper basket. If I had set fire to a loaf of bread or if I had poured out a carton of milk I can see you getting upset, but not for a dollar bill."

The professor would go on. "Rather than feel concerned that I have burned a dollar bill you should be happy. After all, I can no longer enjoy the goods that the dollar could have purchased. Therefore, they are available for others to enjoy, including yourselves. What appears to you like an act of destruction is in fact an act of benevolence. For each dollar I burn I give a dollar of buying power to others."

The same principle that applies to the flamboyant professor applies to the robber barons who used to light their cigars with big bills in a conspicuous demonstration of their affluence. They were also being generous, even if it was the furthest thought from their minds. So too was the airplane hijacker, D. B. Cooper, who jumped with bags of money he had demanded from the airline, much of which was never recovered. It is no surprise that he has a fan club. He shifted wealth to every person holding U.S. dollars at the cost of the airline and/or its insurers.

These unusual circumstances of people burning dollar bills or jumping with them out of airplanes provide a general insight that comes from thinking economically. The examples reveal how money is relevant to an individual but not relevant to society. The national pie is not generally made any smaller by burning money, so society does not suffer. However, those who burn money are made poorer.

The difference between individual and aggregate effects of destroying—or making—money is another example of the important concept of the fallacy of composition which shows that we cannot deduce what is good for society from what is good for each individual member of society, or vice versa. We met this before with the paradox of thrift, where each individual was better off by increasing savings while society was made poorer. We also met the concept in the context of public goods like public television. In the case of money, while each person losing money is poorer, whether it is burned or in some other way destroyed, society is not poorer. We see we must be careful in making aggregate statements based on knowledge of disaggregate effects.

Just to check whether the distributional consequences of changing the money supply are clear to everybody, let us ask what happens if, during a war, boxes of magnificently produced and undetectable bills are dropped from the air to destroy an economy. Let us suppose that the amount dropped is not so great as to cause the public to resort to barter.

Because those dropping the bills do not get to spend them, they gain no economic advantage themselves. Those who do gain economically are those who discover the boxes of phony bills. The gain of the lucky folk who find the money is at the expense of the others, including the government. What happens is that the government's hidden tax collection, which is likely to be particularly large during wartime, doesn't go as far. The government therefore has to resort to printing even more money or raising explicit taxes, like income or corporate taxes, which are unpopular even during war.

The transfer of income or wealth between holders or demanders of money and those making or supplying it is part of a more general transfer caused by inflation. However, unlike the transfer between demanders and suppliers of money, the other transfers do not occur if inflation is correctly anticipated. This conclusion from thinking economically is not obvious. It depends on an appreciation of how anticipated inflation affects interest rates.

Suppose we have been in a situation in which there has been stable prices, that is, zero inflation. Let us assume that in this situation interest rates on default-free government bonds have been steady at 6 percent. All of a sudden, perhaps because of some outside factor such as the surprise election of a government promising spending financed by printing money, suppose that everyone expects inflation of 10 percent. If interest rates stayed at 6 percent, savers would expect to find themselves 4 percent poorer after a year of increasing prices; while each dollar saved will return $1.06, it would take a $1.10 after a year to buy what $1 would previously have purchased. If savers are to receive the same *real return,* that is, the return after inflation, they must earn 16 percent; the $1.16 received after a year with prices up by 10 percent will buy 6 percent more than the dollar that was saved. But are savers likely to receive 16 percent?

Savers will receive 16 percent only if the borrowers will pay this rate. If the borrowers also expect 10 percent inflation, paying 16 percent interest rates on their borrowing will represent only a 6 percent real cost. This is because they pay back the principal borrowed with dollars that have fallen 10 percent in value during the year. It follows that if the borrowers expect 10 percent inflation they should be willing to pay 16 percent. Hence, with savers demanding the extra 10 percent to compensate for inflation, and borrowers prepared to pay the extra 10 percent, the expected rate of inflation should be reflected in the *nominal* or *market* interest rate. In other words, the interest would become 16 percent, with 10 percent being the *inflation premium* and 6 percent being the *real rate of interest.*

If inflation that had generally been expected to be 10 percent turns out to be 10 percent as expected, borrowers do not gain and lenders do not lose. However, if the actual rate of inflation exceeds 10 percent, that is, if there is unanticipated inflation, there is a transfer of wealth. For example, if realized inflation is 14 percent, those saving and getting 16 percent will really get only a 2 percent real return.

However, offsetting this we have the borrowers. While they paid 16 percent, if the dollars used in repayment have depreciated by 14 percent their real interest payment is only 2 percent.

We find that unanticipated inflation of 4 percent (14 percent actual less 10 percent expected) has lowered the return to savers by 4 percent below their anticipated 6 percent. The lenders' loss is, however, the borrowers' gain. They find themselves paying 4 percent less than expected. There is, therefore, a transfer caused by inflation from those saving to those borrowing. However, the transfer is caused by only the unanticipated inflation, not the total inflation. The anticipated inflation is compensated for in interest rates paid and received.

Where are we likely to find these transfers? Unanticipated inflation rewards those who borrowed at fixed interest rates, and it hurts those who saved. Anybody who bought a home before the 1960s would be among the gainers. The inflation that occurred in that decade far exceeded what had been anticipated. Therefore, the mortgage interest rates which were set before the 1960s did not make the homeowners pay the true cost of their borrowed funds. Of course, the homeowners' gain was at the cost of those who put their funds into fixed interest rate loans out of which came the buyers' mortgages.

The biggest losers from unanticipated inflation are those holding long-term fixed coupon bonds. These are sometimes held directly by the public, but are frequently held on behalf of individuals in their pension or other savings plans. When there is unanticipated inflation, interest earnings inside these plans do not compensate for the declining real value of the bonds, and while the value of the plans do grow they do not maintain their real return. This becomes most apparent when the plans are withdrawn on retirement and it is discovered they do not go as far as had been expected. So it is true, as most non-economists believe, that those on pensions lose from inflation, but as the expected inflation is generally compensated within the interest rates earned, it is only unanticipated inflation that really hurts.

It should be pointed out that when there is unanticipated disinflation—when inflation is slower than had been anticipated—those holding bonds for retirement will gain from the situation. For example, if inflation had been expected to be 10 percent and bonds yielding 16 percent had been purchased, if inflation turns out to be only 4 percent, the holders of bonds directly or via pension plans find themselves earning 12 percent per annum after allowing for inflation. According to Rational Expectationists, this outcome of overestimated inflation is as likely as the reverse because rational people are as likely to overestimate as underestimate. It follows, at least to those who believe that expectations are rational, that on average over long periods of time, pensioners or others with savings should not lose from inflation, a conclusion reached by few non-economists.

When we bring in taxes, the situation is more complex. When interest income is taxed, inflation hurts savers unless interest rates increase by more than inflation. For example, if with zero inflation interest rates would have been 6 percent, and people pay income tax of 25 percent, they would earn 4.5 percent after taxes. If inflation increases to 10 percent they need to earn 19.33 percent before taxes to still receive a return of 4.5 percent after taxes. This is because after taxes, but before inflation, they earn $.75 \times 19.33$ percent = 14.5 percent, which after inflation of 10 percent, represents an increase in buying power of 14.5 percent − 10 percent = 4.5 percent, the same as before inflation. Some economists believe that interest rates will go up to keep the real after-tax and after-inflation interest rates constant, but there is no consensus on this question.

Apart from the problem of taxes, we find that unanticipated inflation hurts savers, but unanticipated disinflation helps them. But if the savers are hurt or helped, then the borrowers must correspondingly be helped or hurt, as this is a zero-sum game. For example, when inflation is faster than had been expected, those issuing long-term bonds find themselves repaying with deflated dollars and the interst rate they pay does not compensate for this. But who are the bond issuers who gain? At this point economic thinking truly comes into its own.

Corporations issue bonds and gain from unanticipated inflation but lose from unanticipated disinflation. When the corporations gain, the shareholders of the corporations gain. What the shareholders gain is what the bondholders lose. Hence, unanticipated inflation redistributes the value of a corporation from the bondholders to the shareholders. Unanticipated disinflation, which Rational Expectationists believe to be as common, redistributes wealth from the shareholders to bondholders.

An even more important issuer of bonds than corporations is the government. The national debt of the United States is held by the public in the form of Treasury bills and bonds to the tune of many hundreds of billions of dollars. It follows that when there is unanticipated inflation, the holders of these government bonds lose. But who gains? The government gains. However, because the government is the representative of the people, it is the people that gain.

The people that gain from unanticipated inflation are the taxpayers. This is because the amount they must pay to *service* the national debt—the interest and principal repayments—is reduced in real terms by unanticipated inflation. Thus, the loss of the holders of government bonds is the gain of the taxpayers. This is another redistribution of wealth caused by unanticipated inflation that few without training in economics would realize, namely that unanticipated inflation helps taxpayers.

While it might help taxpayers via the retiring of the national debt the effect of unanticipated inflation might be swamped by the effect of total inflation, whether unanticipated or not, on income tax rates. This is because without *indexation* higher fractions of incomes should be paid in taxes at higher incomes as a result of the tax structure being *progressive*. It is only from *un*anticipated inflation that taxpayers gain. Even then, the government might not use the windfall from the reduced real amount owed on the national debt to reduce tax rates. If instead they spend more, it is those receiving what they spend who gain rather than taxpayers.

The effect of unanticipated inflation on the real value of the national debt has important implications for the calculation of the fiscal deficit. According to most people's thinking, the fiscal deficit is the amount by which the national debt increases during each year because the financing of the deficit involves the selling of bonds or other claims on the government.

The interest paid by the government on its Treasury bills and bonds is included in most published accounts as an expenditure of the government in the same way as the accounts record other expenditures, such as education and defense. An increase in anticipated inflation will increase the interest expense because much of the debt is short term—Treasury bills—and is constantly being renewed, or *refinanced*. This means that as inflation increases and is anticipated to increase, the government is forced to run larger deficits as conventionally calculated. But are they really larger? Economic thinking indicates a problem here.

As we have already mentioned, inflation lowers the real value of the outstanding national debt. For example, if the national debt is $1,500 billion, 10 percent inflation would lower the real value of the national debt by $150 billion during a year. However, the interest paid on the debt that compensates for inflation is included in the calculation of the deficit, while the benefit in terms of the real debt retired is not. A strong case can be made that the $150 billion benefit from retirement of the real national debt should be subtracted from the fiscal deficit, or alternatively, that we should not include as an expenditure that part of interest that corresponds to anticipated inflation.

It is not only for government deficits that we should make adjustments for inflation. The same is true for the calculation of corporate deficits or profits, as the real value of corporate debt is also reduced by unanticipated inflation. If we include the payment of interest as a current corporate expense, but do not allow for the real retirement of debt, we show profits that are lower than they really are. Either we should not include the inflation premium component of interest payments as an expense, or we should add to revenues the benefits of the outstanding debt that is retired by inflation. Accountants do not make these adjustments, but buyers of stocks may be making them anyway in determining what to pay for different stocks.

THINKING BIG

Many non-economists have a better appreciation than economists about the consequences of unemployment because economists, especially those with university tenure, are themselves rarely unemployed. However, if we were to compare the thinking of employed economists with that of non-economists who have not experienced the indignity and degradation of unemployment, we might find an important difference.

Non-economists tend to think of unemployment and inflation as comparably evil. Both are believed to do about the same amount of harm and therefore to be equally worth banishing. Economists know that inflation and unemployment impose very different costs in terms of human suffering. Inflation, especially if it is anticipated, has little effect. It is compatible with increasing prosperity, and provided incomes and prices are increasing at equal rates, nobody need lose. Even inflation that is unanticipated merely redistributes wealth and does not destroy it. Gains match losses in a zero-sum game.

Unemployment is a very different problem from inflation. The work that is not done by the unemployed is never recaptured. The goods and service that could have been made are gone forever. This is in addition to the indignity involved. There is no way that an economist would say that a reduction in inflation of "x" percent is worthwhile if it causes up to "y" percent more unemployment. This, they argue, is a political decision, and economists believe they are supposed to limit their thinking to positive questions. What economists are prepared to explain is whether there is a payoff in terms of lower inflation by having more unemployment. As we have shown, Monetarists think this payoff is highly questionable, especially in the long run, and if

Rational Expectationists are correct, there may not even be a systematic short-run payoff.

While economists are not generally prepared to choose between inflation and unemployment, economic thinking can throw important light on the effect of these two maladies on the fiscal deficit. We have seen how inflation impacts on the deficit and the corrections that it suggests, so we should also see how unemployment affects the fiscal deficit.

When there is unemployment, incomes are low; therefore, income tax receipts of government are reduced. At the same time, automatic increases in spending by government take place on such items as unemployment compensation and welfare benefits. The lower taxes and higher spending increase the calculated fiscal deficit.

When we are comparing fiscal deficits to see in which years fiscal policy has been the most stimulatory, we have to make adjustments for these effects of unemployment. For example, observing a large deficit in a year when there is heavy unemployment does not necessarily indicate that the government was intending to expand the economy. In order to judge how expansionary the government intended to be, we must calculate the deficits at a common level of unemployment to eliminate the effects of unemployment on the measured deficits. This requires selecting a common level of unemployment—usually the *full-employment level*—then estimating what the deficits would have been had this level of unemployment prevailed in each year. This calculation is difficult and involves working out how much more in taxes would have been collected if full employment had occurred, and how much lower government spending would have been. The resulting deficit when put on a full employment basis is called the *full employment deficit*.

THINKING BIG

At this juncture, you might well be thinking that economic thinking is dangerous. It can turn large deficits into small deficits and can even turn a big deficit into a surplus. Bear in mind, however, that these implications of economic thinking are important for policy makers to appreciate. Otherwise, we might find ourselves trying to balance the budget when there is heavy unemployment, which is a very dangerous thing to do, and might not be necessary if inflation is retiring a large outstanding national debt. It is more important that policy makers think economically than the person in the street, but the policy makers are more likely to think economically if they know the voters are also thinking economically.

PART IV

THINKING
ALOUD

The Horizons and
Limitations of Economics

CHAPTER 17

Thinking Openly

International Trade and Finance

> The mind is like a parachute; it functions only when it's open.
> **Anonymous**
>
> It is good to have an open mind, but be sure it is not open at both ends.
> **Anonymous**

WHEN it comes to international economics, which is sometimes referred to as *open-economy economics,* the thinking of non-economists and economists can be further apart than the nations involved in international trade. So many myths have gained popular currency that they have even molded international economic policy.

A commonly held myth, subscribed to by many a non-economist, is that quotas and tariffs on imports protect jobs and thereby keep incomes higher than they would have been without them. The basis of this belief is that by keeping out goods and services that compete with those produced domestically we preserve markets and, therefore, jobs. Quotas keep foreign products out by directly limiting the number that can be imported while tariffs work by making foreign produced items more expensive. So well established is the belief that quotas and tariffs protect jobs that we are surrounded by examples of both. At different times we have seen them on footwear, television sets, automobiles, trucks, and steel.

Economic thinking leads us to conclude that while a quota or tariff may help protect jobs in those sectors specifically protected, and may thereby increase incomes of people in those jobs, overall they make people poorer. The basis of this conclusion is the Theory of Comparative Advantage, which was initially advanced by the economist David Ricardo early in the nineteenth century.

According to this theory, each country should specialize in producing those items in which it has a *comparative advantage,* even though this might mean producing items in which other countries have an *absolute advantage*. The meaning of comparative advantage, and the reason for the conclusion, can be revealed by the following example:

If the United States is a more expensive producer of both cars and computers than Japan, but is only a little more expensive at producing computers and much more expensive at producing cars, then according to Ricardo's theory the United States should produce computers while Japan should produce cars. This is because the United States has a comparative advantage producing computers even though it has an absolute disadvantage in producing both cars and computers. By comparative advantage, we mean only that relative to other products that the United States could produce, it is more cost-effective to produce computers. Cost effectiveness is judged not in terms of dollars or yen, but in terms of the number of people or machines required to produce a given output.

At first thought, it might appear odd that the United States should or would produce anything if it has an absolute disadvantage in both products. But here is the reason for the conclusion of the Theory of Comparative Advantage. It is better for people and machines in the United States to be producing something rather than be idle. And if they are to produce something, it is better that they are busy making whatever they are relatively better at doing. Then, with everyone employed both in the United States and Japan, global output will be higher. There will then be some distribution of this output whereby people in both countries are better off.

The problem with tariffs and quotas is that they cause countries to produce items for which they do not have a comparative advantage. If there is a sufficient tariff on automobiles entering the United States, it will pay to produce more of them in the U.S. than there should be according to the criteria of efficiency. Similarly, if Japan put a quota or tariff on U.S.-produced computers it would encourage production in Japan at the expense of the U.S. If this example doesn't make it apparent, think of tariffs on coffee or mangoes. Surely, these should be grown where there are favorable conditions for growing them, but with a sufficient tariff or restrictive quota you can bet it would be worth producing them, even in Canada or the United States.

While tariffs and quotas make us collectively poorer they clearly help the protected workers. For example, auto workers will earn more if imported cars face tariffs. Furthermore, because domestic auto producers compete with imports, they too can charge more because of tariffs and quotas. However, consumers will pay more for imported cars than they would have without tariffs. So while selective workers and the auto industry gain from import restrictions, all car buyers are worse off. Indeed, because the restrictions hurt in the aggregate, any gain by domestic auto workers and companies must be more than offset by losses incurred by foreign producers and by consumers everywhere.

To the extent that competition within a country is limited by restrictions on car imports, the owners or shareholders of protected firms gain as well as the workers. This is because new entrants will not compete away the profits from protection. However, the owners of some firms may not be residents of the country imposing the protective measures. What frequently happens is that foreign firms locate inside a country to avail themselves of tariff protection. A Japanese or European auto maker may open a U.S. plant to avoid import restrictions.

It is worth pointing out that economic thinking on the question of ownership can help us debunk another myth that is only indirectly related to international competition and import restrictions. Many people without economic training believe that if, for instance, a U.S. car firm or any other manufacturer went bankrupt all the jobs in the company would be lost. Economists realize that as long as the plants remain, as physically they will, the effect of bankruptcy is different ownership. For some price of the failed company's assets it would pay a different owner, perhaps a foreign company with good managers, to run the failed company's plants profitably. Bankruptcy does not mean plants disappear, but merely means different ownership and generally better corporate management, and is therefore not a reason for bailouts, which primarily help the shareholders.

There are limited circumstances in which economic thinking can be used to support restrictions on imports.

Perhaps the most persuasive involves the *infant-industry argument,* which is that restrictions can help while a new industry gets off the ground. This argument is clearly valid, and without some form of trade protection many industries, including many in Japan, would not have reached their level of prominence, if they survived at all. The only problem with infants is removing the protection when they grow up.

A relevant argument for protection can be based on defense. Strategic considerations do not allow a nation to import certain important items that make them vulnerable in the event of a war. By no means unrelated to this argument is the case for tariffs and quotas to keep an economy diversified. Even in the absence of wars, changes in relative demands make countries vulnerable if they depend on a limited variety of products. The benefits of diversification are not recognized or internalized by individual firms, and therefore, as we mentioned in chapter 10, governments may be tempted to provide subsidies. The diversity argument is most commonly heard in resource-based nations where volatile movements in prices of their exports versus imports—known as the *terms of trade*—cause great variations in the standard of living.

Economic thinking throws important light on the meaning of balance of trade surpluses and deficits. While most non-economists know that a trade surplus means that exports exceed imports, few non-economists realize that surpluses are not a good thing to consistently record.

When a nation exports more than it imports it is producing more goods and services for others to consume than it consumes in return of other nations' goods and services. But why should a nation do this when it means enjoying a standard of living lower than its production level warrants?

When a nation has a trade surplus it is receiving in payment for its exports more than it is paying out for imports. This means it is adding to its holdings of gold or foreign exchange. What a surplus in the trade balance means, then, is that the country's goods are being exchanged for gold or paper currencies of other countries. For instance, when the United States was running trade surpluses as it was many years ago, it was exporting its manufacturing and agricultural output in return for gold and pieces of colored paper decorated with pictures of other nations' heroes. Moreover, because most foreign exchange is held in foreign bank accounts, when the U.S. was running trade surpluses it was getting increased ledger entries in foreign banks rather than gold or attractive foreign notes.

Accumulating gold and foreign bank accounts is not a bad idea if they are used later. However, this means that the country that runs surpluses should later run trade deficits. Of course, they shouldn't run deficits for too long or they will get into debt, as indeed the United States began to do in the 1980s. Therefore, we discover that economic thinking suggests nations should balance trade over a period of years. Surpluses should be followed by deficits, and vice versa, with the average deficit/surplus being zero.

Closely related to the economists' way of thinking about balance of trade deficits and surpluses is their way of thinking about effects of international movements of capital. Non-economists might be tempted to think that an inflow of capital is beneficial, whereas economic thinking leads us to a different conclusion.

Capital can flow into a nation via the purchase of *debt*, that is, via investment in bills and bonds, or via the purchase of *equity,* that is, stocks or property. Therefore, there might be a benefit to the sellers of debt or equity during the period when the capital flows in. However in all subsequent periods, interest must be paid on debt, and dividends/rent paid on equity. The once-and-for-all benefit will be followed by a steady drain that appears as an outflow of *services* in the balance of payments. The services referred to are debt-service and equity-service, and these cause monies to leave a nation just like the purchase of any other imported service like travel, shipping, consulting, insurance, and so on.

When an inflow of capital is used for an investment that would not otherwise have occurred, the drain of interest and dividends may be offset by foreign earnings from the investment. If funds flowed into Canada to develop Arctic or East Coast oil the revenue from the oil could cover the required interest or dividend payments. The problem from capital inflows is, therefore, from not investing the funds and instead using them for consumption. Indeed, there are numerous examples of Latin and Central American nations where funds borrowed from overseas went into subsidizing consumption rather than into financing investment. There was hence no offsetting income to cover payments to service the overseas loans. The developing countries' debt crisis of the 1980s comes to mind when we think of overseas funds being used for consumption.

Just as many non-economists think balance of payments surpluses are good, they also tend to think that increases in the foreign exchange value of a nation's currency—referred to as a *revaluation,* or *appreciation*—are good. In this case the non-economist may be correct, but economic thinking tells us that an increased currency value can be problematic.

THINKING ALOUD

On the good side, when the foreign exchange value of a currency increases it buys more foreign goods. This means that consumers who have that currency enjoy an improvement in their standard of living via being able to afford more imports. This improvement in standard of living can also be seen if we calculate the income levels of different nations, converting them into a common currency for comparison. The incomes of peoples whose currencies have increased in value will convert into more of the measurement currency, vaulting their "corrected" income up the national income comparison ladder.

While consumers are better off from an increase in the value of their currency, producers will be worse off. Just as imports become cheaper from an increased currency value, so exports become more expensive for foreigners to buy. Exporters therefore find it more difficult to sell when their currency increases in value. The more price-sensitive foreign buyers are, which is in turn determined by the availability of local substitutes, the more exporters are hurt.

Increases in a currency's value also hurt people who have invested abroad in certain financial instruments. The increased value of their own currency means overseas investments are not worth as much when converted into their currency. On the other hand, those who have foreign debt denominated in foreign currency find their liabilities have been reduced when converted into their currency. We again find a mixed set of effects that might not be apparent to many non-economists.

Closely connected to the mixed effects of an increased currency value is the effect of the discovery of a major resource in a country. It might well seem, for example, that finding oil off the British coast, or natural gas off the Dutch coast, would bring nothing but economic benefits, but the reality can be different.

When exchange rates are free to move with market forces, the discovery of oil or gas can cause an appreciation in the value of the discovering country's currency. However, as we have seen, this hurts exporters. What we therefore find is the bonanza of oil or gas hurting traditional industries, which find it more difficult to compete. Some of these industries fail, victims of what has been called the *Dutch disease,* deriving from the economic dislocation in some Dutch industries after the discovery of vast amounts of natural gas off their coast.

With all the inflation and international crises seen during the twentieth century, many non-economists and even some economists argue that we need to return to the system of international exchange that was prevalent in the nineteenth century, the gold standard.

The gold standard involved each country fixing, or *pegging,* the value of its paper currency in terms of gold. For instance, dollars might have been pegged at one-fortieth of an ounce of fine gold, while British pounds might have been pegged at one-twentieth of an ounce. What these values mean is that it takes $40 to buy an ounce of gold in the United States, and £20 in Britain. But how can a government ensure that these prices will prevail?

In order to prevent the price of gold in the United States exceeding $40 per ounce, it would be necessary for the government or some appointed agent like the Federal Reserve always to stand ready to sell at that price. Then no one could ever charge more than $40 or people would buy from the government. Similarly, in order to ensure that the price of gold never falls below $40 per ounce, the government must stand ready to buy at this price. Every country on the gold-standard system must behave in this way, redeeming and selling its paper money for gold.

If gold costs $40 per ounce in the United States and £20 per ounce in Britain, the exchange rate between dollars and pounds will be approximately $2 for each pound sterling. The reason is that if the exchange rate were something else, say, $2.20 per pound sterling, it would be profitable to *arbitrage*. For example, a person could take £1, buy $2.20 of U.S. paper money at the assumed exchange rate and use this to buy 2.20/40 = .055 ounces of gold at $40 per ounce in the United States. The gold could be shipped to London and sold at £20 per ounce, fetching £1.10. As the person doing this started with only £1 he or she would be richer without taking a risk. Many people would therefore do the arbitrage, selling their pounds for dollars, until the pound had fallen in value to only $2.00. Of course, there is a small range within which the exchange rate can move because of costs of shipping gold and exchanging currencies, but it is relatively narrow.

This explains how the gold standard worked and determined the exchange rates, but why is it still so popular with non-economists and some economists? It is because when a government must stand prepared to sell gold at a fixed price it must limit the amount of paper money in circulation. If there is too much paper money there could be more currency coming in for conversion than the government can redeem in gold. This imposes a discipline on the central bank.

A further factor favoring the gold standard concerns its implications for the automatic elimination of deficits in the balance of payments. As we have stated, when a country runs a balance of payments deficit, its residents are spending more abroad than non-residents are spending in that country. If the countries settle their imbalances in gold this means that the deficit countries must ship gold to those running surpluses. This means the deficit countries have declining gold reserves encouraging their governments to reduce the amount of paper money in circulation, while the reverse is happening in the surplus countries. This means deflation, or at least slower inflation, in the deficit countries than in the surplus countries, certainly if we subscribe to the Quantity Theory of Money explained earlier. With slower inflation in the deficit countries than elsewhere their goods become increasingly competitive so their exports increase while their imports decline with residents substituting their own products. Consequently, the deficits are reduced via what is often called the *price-specie adjustment mechanism,* an automatic mechanism working via prices and gold (that is, specie) to restore international balance.

So much for the positive side of the gold standard. While many economists see these benefits of making gold the basis of an international financial system, they also recognize that there is a major problem in gold which is not generally appreciated by the public.

Gold is expensive to mine and use as a reserve. It takes resources to dig it out of the ground, and even after it has been mined it must be smelted into bars and flown under heavy, expensive security to places like the New York Federal Reserve Bank. When it arrives it is put back into the ground and protected at great expense—a waste of resources. Add to this the fact that the largest producers of gold are South Africa and the Soviet Union, hardly favorites with the United States, and there is solid reason to look for an alternative.

Another international question on which it helps to think economically concerns the effect of speculation on volatility of exchange rates. Non-economists invariably hold the view that speculators are a destabilizing influence who manipulate markets and make exchange rates more unstable than they would have been. The image is of greedy types in gold-rimmed spectacles and pin-striped suits making fat profits by moving massive amounts of money without regard to the effects it has on the value of currencies.

Economists realize that speculation can be destabilizing only if speculators lose money. In order to see why this is so, let us think of destabilization as meaning that exchange rates go higher than they would have gone when they are high, and lower than they would have gone when they are low, than if there had not been currency speculation.

For a currency to go higher than it would have gone when it is already high, speculators must be buying it. For it to go lower than it would have gone when it is already low, speculators must be selling it. This means that to be destabilizing, speculators must buy high and sell low, a sure way to lose money. The only way speculators can make profits is by buying currencies when they are low, meaning they don't go as low as they would otherwise have gone, and selling when they are high, meaning they don't go as high as they would otherwise have gone. Hence, successful stabilization means that exchange rates move within a narrower range than in speculation's absence, the opposite to what many non-economists think.

According to economic thinking, it is when currencies are backed by a reserve that speculation is destabilizing. To see this, let us again consider the gold standard. Suppose that by seeing statistics showing a declining gold reserve speculators decide that a central bank is going to devalue. This means lowering the value of its money by increasing the amount of it that is needed to buy gold. To avoid losing money, the speculators will cash in their paper currency and get gold. But this will make the gold reserves lower. This will increase the perception that a devaluation is likely and cause even more to convert paper to gold. Eventually the central bank will run out of gold and will be forced to devalue, even if the original reason for the damaging speculation had not been valid.

The foregoing examples make it clear how different the conclusions reached by thinking economically about international economics can be. They should also show that learning to think economically can come considerably more quickly than learning to think in a foreign language.

CHAPTER 18

Thinking Conclusively

The Limitations of Economic Thinking

A conclusion is a place where you get tired thinking.
MARTIN FISCHER

And the moral of that is—"The more there is of mine, the less there is of yours."
LEWIS CARROLL,
Alice's Adventures in Wonderland

IT IS PERHAPS remarkable that some of the questions non-economists think economists think about most have not been tackled by economists at all. In this account of how they think we have not tackled such questions as why this or that person, or this or that nation is richer than some other person or nation. Why have the Fords, Vanderbilts, and others done so well, and why is the United States so much richer than countries in South America, some of which have almost as many resources? Why is Japan making such rapid advances in living standards? How can *you* become rich? Surely these questions must be what many non-economists believe economic thinking helps us answer.

Questions of relative wealth and relative incomes are *distributional* questions. In other sciences distribution is at the center of interest. In physics it is the focus of the second law of thermodynamics, which claims that the distribution of energy becomes more even over time. If we have two cylinders of water joined at the bottom by a tube with a valve, and we open it, the cylinder with the highest potential energy loses it, and the other gains it. Only when the energy distribution is even does the redistribution stop. Or if we have two bodies with different heat, the warmer body will provide heat to the colder body until temperatures are even. (Indeed, due to the fact that the conservation of energy was initially studied with heat, the law became known as a thermodynamic law.)

In chemistry, distribution is the basis of the kinetic theory of gases in which the distribution of molecular energy is studied. In astronomy, it is recognized that as far as we know the universe exhibits an evening out of the distribution of energy, or in the jargon of the scientist, increasing entropy.

In medicine, epidemiologists know that diseases are distributed in remarkably predictable patterns and at pre-dictable rates. Even in political science, the distribution of political power and the formation of coalitions to effect the power distribution are essential to a way of thinking.

Despite the central place of distribution in most other sciences, when it comes to economics distribution is given very little attention. There is no law subscribed to by most economists that is equivalent to the law of increasing entropy, saying, for example, that if wealth is spread unevenly among people or countries, that it will eventually be distributed evenly. Indeed, Marxists who study distributional questions, but who are not considered to be economists by economists, claim that the distribution would become even more uneven. They claim that eventually it would become so uneven that there will be revolution—equivalent to a big bang—and that it would then become more even in a peoples' socialism.

Isn't there some theory in economics in which the rich become apathetic and the poor work harder so that their different levels of ambition eventually equalize the distribution of income and wealth? Or how about some theory that rich nations are those that have most land, most tolerance to ethnic diversity, most devotion to free enterprise, or the smallest fraction of GNP consumed or generated by government? And as distribution is affected and effected by government decisions, what is it that makes governments select particular types of income or profits taxes, minimum wage laws, rent controls, and other ways of helping some people at the expense of others? Surely a full explanation of what we observe requires that we explain some of these redistributional programs that are popular in many different countries.

The fact that society does reallocate income from what random endowments would have caused has not drawn economists into studying distributional questions because this involves normative decisions. Taxes and subsidies are aimed at achieving an allocation of income that the government thinks ought to occur, and "ought" questions are not amenable to the economist's way of thinking. Economists believe they cannot explain why many governments believe that people should pay only "reasonable" rents, earn "reasonable" wages, receive "reasonable" prices for their agricultural output, enjoy "reasonable" job security, and so on. However, while these do involve normative decisions economists cannot ignore them. Making them exogenous leaves a picture or model that displays only part of our economic landscape.

Perhaps even more remarkable than the absence of theories of distribution in economics is the prevalent attitude to changes in whatever status quo distribution factor endowments have caused. The attitude of most economists is that any attempt to interfere with the status quo distributions of income would make things worse. This is true about minimum wage laws to help the poor, rent controls to help renters, tariffs to protect jobs, food stamps to help the hungry, and virtually every program government has ever devised. But what is behind this tendency for economists to draw negative conclusions about schemes to help the disadvantaged, and their consequent tendency to favor unregulated markets and the survival of the fittest?

We can provide an explanation of the attitude of economists to anything but the natural order if we draw a parallel between the subject matter of the biological—note the "logic" in the name—and the economic sciences. This reveals not only remarkably similar subject matter, but also a common pattern for the majority of scientists in these coextensive disciplines to hold the philosophical opinion that the best environment is the untouched, natural environment.

Biologists, like economists, are interested in gains from the division of labor. The biologist notes how individual bees in a hive specialize in working, defending, nursing, and reproducing. They also describe how termites divide up their labor allowing adaptation of individuals within a colony so that soldiers, builders, and so on, have a physical character suited to their role. In a remarkably similar way, economists note how we specialize in teaching, nursing, soldiering, housekeeping, and writing books in economics. They note how by doing this we develop our skills and share our improved output via the marketplace, just as bees and termites share their collective effort via some programmed co-operation.

It is not only within colonies of insects that biologists observe specialization. Division of labor is also found within biological entities. Trees are made up of leaves that collect light and produce sugars and trunks that carry water to leaves and hold them in the sunlight. Humans have front teeth for biting, back teeth for chewing, feet for walking, hands for holding and touching, and so on. Evolution has ensured that we are efficiently organized for our environment, and that we can get maximum output from the energy we put in. In a similar way, economists note how firms combine inputs to produce a given output for the least cost, or get the most output from a given input. Moreover, it is only the fittest firms that survive competition, just as only the fittest animals and plants survive in their harsh environments.

Biologists and economists also think remarkably alike about the effects of exogenous changes. As the biological environment changes, the biologist can predict with some degree of accuracy how this will affect the plants and animals. Colder weather favors animals with fur and plants that can survive frost. Increased rain favors plants needing water while drying trends encourage the plants of the desert. The selection of prospering biological varieties is at least in part determined by mutation in the transfer of genetic information from generation to generation.

The analogous adaptation principle to mutation found in economics is innovation, with the relatively rare successful innovation setting the stage for the next generation of firms. Competition forces out those who do not innovate just as the struggle for survival in a scarce environment favors those biological species with particular mutations.

Even the alternative evolutionary model to that of Darwin and known as the Lamarckian model, in which the required variations in structure appear when most needed, has its parallel in economics. Imitation based on others' successful innovations and the search for new products and methods when others fail is clearly consistent with Lamarckian principles.

There is another striking parallel between biology and economics that is apparent in a modern development in both fields, the role of socialization in our survival. Biologists have become aware that we have been programmed by evolution not so much to advance or preserve ourselves individually, but to advance or preserve our genes. For example, when a seagull finds food it not only feeds itself and its young, but it announces to other gulls by its loud scream that it has discovered food. Of course, this lowers the chance of this particular seagull surviving because the arrival of other gulls causes it to share. So why do gulls still scream when they find food? The answer provided by sociobiologists is that the species has survived because they scream, thereby making use of more food. This social behavior, which might be described as being "mutual altruism," has, despite the freeloader incentive to personally remain quiet while letting the others still do the screaming, become programmed into gulls by evolution. Screaming is socially beneficial but individually costly, and for some evolutionary or as yet unknown reason the social behavior eventually dominates. The same is true of screaming in self-defense. This sometimes draws predators away from others carrying the same genotype, helping the genotype survive.

The tendency for species to adapt so as to protect their genes is also apparent in the numerous stories of mothers risking their lives to save their children. This is observed in a vast variety of animal species.

Just as in the field of sociobiology we find the maximization of the survival of the species rather than the individual, so in economics we find the maximization of household rather than individual utility. This implies altruism within the family and has important implications for explaining what we observe. For example, the fact that households make decisions of what to consume helps to explain the popularity of bland products. This is because when any individual member of the household holds a veto on a decision, whether it be to see a movie with a well-known star who some like and others don't, or to eat spicy food, it is the lowest common denominator that wins the day. Furthermore, the fact that societies have managed to generate a consensus to make investments that benefit primarily future generations—such as the planting of trees or a declaration of a national park—suggests that via the political apparatus the utility of society, a very broad altruism, does matter in an individual's decisions.

Almost certainly the strongest commonality between biologists and economists is their shared appreciation of the interdependence of the units they study. Within biology the entire field of ecology is devoted to studying complex interdependencies. Anybody who has read Rachel Carson's *The Edge of the Sea* will immediately appreciate how the ecosystems of tidepools and beaches are themselves like living organisms made up of separate organisms. There is a remarkable balance and harmony, with each of the parts cooperating to support the entity without any central planning or conscious control as in the competitive equilibrium (or harmony) in economics.

The interdependence of units in our highly specialized economy, where individual producers and consumers without central control keep us fed and clothed, might be considered as remarkable as that in ecological environments. For example, food reaches tables in a largely urbanized society where few farm, with the principle of exchange being the economist's equivalent of the biological principle of mutualism. Via the mechanism of prices and the quest for profit we find farmers producing, shippers carrying, wholesalers distributing, and retailers selling what we want. Somehow or other it works. No unit is self-sufficient, but collectively we cooperate without coercion and conscious guidances so that our desires are satisfied.

The "invisible hand" is as apt a description of the forces guiding and coordinating the biological environment as it is for that of the economy for which Adam Smith, who was aware of the connection with biology, coined the term. What might have been chaos turns out to be a harmonious interplay among units that are unconscious participants in the ecosystem, whether "eco" be short for *eco*logy or *eco*nomics.

Ecosystems in our natural and economic environments are more stable the more diversity they represent in their overall structure. Just as there are rewards to the individual from a diversified portfolio of risky investments so it is in the biological environment where mankind's selection of individual varieties of, for instance, wheat and trees to optimize output makes the outcome more open to disaster than the natural order. Optimization doesn't always pay in a risky environment. This knowledge, which has been so carefully refined by professors of finance, has obvious carryovers to biology. More variety may pay even if the average or expected yield—of harvest or investment—is lower.

It is most probably the appreciation of the marvels of the natural order that has been responsible for economists as well as biologists steering clear of trying to alter it. There is a common respect for what occurs without man's intervention and a common belief that virtually any intervention is wrong. History is replete with examples to confirm this. In economics we have the unemployment resulting from well-intended minimum wage laws and the shortage of rental accommodation following rent control. In biology we have some equally celebrated cases.

When the sea otter on the west coast of the United States was shot for its fur, the abalone, the stable of the otters' diet, quickly multiplied. But abalone eat kelp weed and so kelp beds diminished. Herring lay their eggs in kelp so herring populations dwindled. With fewer herring the stock of salmon went down. With interdependencies such as these there is a strong aversion not to fool around with Mother Nature.

Even evolution itself is slowed if altruism within any species, or the building blocks of life, biological cells, supports mutations that are ill-favored or even dangerous to others. Then the successful mutations not only must share their

270

energy to support others, but in succeeding cells of homeostatic entities, genotypes will persist and even thrive that are ill-suited to conditions. The parallel in economics is what is behind advancing prosperity, namely economic growth. Bailouts of unsuccessful innovations have allowed firms to survive that should have failed. The burden to other firms are the higher taxes that drain away their base for further investment.

With history so full of examples where any interference in the economy or ecology has done much harm it is no surprise that economists and biologists have been conservatives/conservationists. Rather than incorporate the political and social factors which have interfered in the natural order to affect redistributions, economists have contented themselves with measuring income distribution.

The inequality of income within a nation can be measured by what fraction of households earn more than each particular income. Indices can be defined that reflect the extent of inequality, and these can be used to see whether it is different between countries or whether it has been changing over time. There is a tendency to think of inequality as bad, although few economists will actually say so. Moreover, some are quick to point out that income and happiness are not necessarily related, and that some inequality may be good because it leaves an incentive for people to move ahead. Moreover, they might tell us that inequality from the past has provided us with natural treasures that would otherwise not have been produced. (Think of the stately homes and castles the public can enjoy in Europe because of unequal distributions long ago, suggesting that inequality of income is bad to have today but good to have had yesterday.)

Unfortunately for the conservatives in economics and the

conservationists in biology, in reality people have altered their natural environment. They have turned some of the wilderness into cities, with roads, shopping centers, homes, and schools, reducing the habitat of wild plants and animals. Indeed, it is the very nature of humans to change their environment to suit their needs and this is what sets them aside from other creatures. And so it is for the economic environment. We have not opted for a society of economic anarchy; instead we have, via our socialized instincts and desire for social justice, managed to construct a society in which we do care for others. Indeed, we have collectively opted for frequently socialized modes of providing social justice. We have provided help for the handicapped and elderly, Medicare, safety regulations, and so on. People are making normative choices and if we are to explain our economic environment we cannot avoid explaining these normative decisions involving redistribution. Social tastes are impacting on our choices and to take them as beyond economics via a statement of *de gustibus non est disputandum,* or tastes cannot be disputed, is to exclude a lot of what affects us. Because normative choices involve social and political goals and determination procedures, including the electoral system, these should be taken into account.

It is because we all do think politically and socially that people have drawn their own conclusions on the broader question about whether to favor intervention or laissez-faire. And it is remarkable how diverse peoples' conclusions have been with extremely conservative and extremely liberal economists all observing the same data base.

What we are saying here is nothing new. Indeed, it was "political economy" that preceded the study of the much narrower subject of economics. Rather, we are arguing for a needed reunification of the currently separate fields in social science and its coextensive subject, biology. We need to make the methods of making our choices endogenous by putting them within our economic model, and we need the economic components of our model to interact with the political components, and vice versa. The interaction is a social question. A model of thinking economically should be—no, we cannot help making normative statements—a broad-based sociopolitical economic model or we will never explain what we are observing, that is, the reality all around us. But does this need to think politically and socially, as well as to think economically, make the solution beyond us? Is the model more complex than we could hope to build and comprehend, however hard we try?

Astronomers began with nothing more than a dark ceiling above them revealing tiny specks of white light. By patient and careful observation and the application of logic, they developed a picture of the scale and structure of the universe. While the astronomer's picture is still being drawn (and perhaps always will be), the work of the scientist has moved slowly and unevenly toward improved knowledge. And so we may hope for economics, that some day we may look back on the accumulation of economic understanding and know we too have come a long way.

INDEX

Index

Index

Index